ESL/EFL

SPEAKING ACTIVITIES
FOR TEENAGERS AND ADULTS
B1 TO C1

REAL LIFE CONVERSATION MATERIAL FOR BUSY TEACHERS

BY POWERPRINT PUBLISHERS

©2023 POWERPRINT PUBLISHERS
All rights reserved.
ISBN 9798371504159

TABLE OF CONTENTS

INTERPERSONAL RELATIONS	5
WORK	14
MEDICINE AND HEALTH	23
FOOD	31
TRAVEL AND TOURISM	38
HOUSE AND HOME	49
SPORTS	57
SCIENCE AND TECHNOLOGY	65
ENVIRONMENT AND NATURE	74
SCHOOL	80
— POLITICS AND SOCIETY	87
SHOPPING AND FASHION	98
— THE MEDIA	106
CULTURE	110

POWERPRINT PUBLISHERS

INTERPERSONAL RELATIONS
DESCRIBE THE PICTURE AND ANSWER THE QUESTIONS

1. Are multigenerational family households popular in your country? Consider advantages and disadvantages of several generations living together.
2. Describe your family. How many generations live together? How are you getting on?

Work in pairs

PERSON "A" SPEAKS FOR A MINUTE ON A GIVEN TOPIC. PERSON "B" ASKS WH-QUESTIONS TO LEARN MORE DETAILS. TAKE TURNS.

Talk about:
- A family member you have the best relationship with.
- A friend you consider a family member.
- A person you lost contact with.
- Characteristics of a good family.
- The best memory connected with a family member.
- Generational gap in your family.
- Reasons for people to get married.
- An appropriate age for men and women to get married.
- An appropriate age for men and women to become parents.

INTERPERSONAL RELATIONS
DESCRIBE THE PICTURE AND ANSWER THE QUESTIONS

1. What is the most popular model of a family in your country? How has the situation changed over the years?
2. Describe the best holiday you have ever had with your family.

Work in pairs

DO YOU AGREE WITH THE STATEMENTS? DISCUSS AND DECIDE.

1. Most people panic in life and death emergency situations.
2. Most people want to move out from home as early as they can.
3. Most people communicate using technology rather than in person.
4. You can choose your friends but you cannot choose your family.
5. In-laws can never become as close as parents.
6. The best place for elderly people to spend the rest of their lives is a residential home.
7. Money is what breaks down families.
8. Nurture not nature decides about person's character.
9. Adoption is a much better option than in-vitro.
10. Children who have siblings are much happier than only children.

INTERPERSONAL RELATIONS
DESCRIBE THE PICTURE AND ANSWER THE QUESTIONS

1. What do you think the people are laughing at?
2. Do you think having meals together strengthens bonds? Do you eat meals together with your family? Why? Why not?
3. Describe some family traditions you cultivate.

Work in pairs

SPECULATE ABOUT THE FUTURE. DO YOU AGREE WITH THE SENTENCES? IN TWENTY YEARS' TIME...

1. The number of people getting divorced will double.
2. Very few people will decide to have children.
3. The birth rate will go down drastically.
4. Life expectancy will increase.
5. Work will be more important than having a family.
6. Homeschooling will be forbidden.
7. There will be one international language instead of national languages.
8. People will be citizens of the world rather than citizens of a particular country.
9. Social media will no longer be popular.
10. People will be able to live as avatars.

INTERPERSONAL RELATIONS
DESCRIBE THE PICTURES AND ANSWER THE QUESTIONS

1. Which of the three pictures shows the healthiest way to sleep? Why?
2. What are the advantages and disadvantage of sleeping alone and with a spouse? What about pets? Should they be allowed to sleep in the owner's bed?
3. Can allowing kids to sleep with parents backfire later on?
4. What should a proper sleep routine look like?
5. What can be done if someone suffers from insomnia or nightmares?
6. Do you think working night shifts interferes with people's sleep pattern?
7. Do you like to sleep in complete darkness and silence?
8. Do you struggle to fall asleep in a new place?
9. Are you an early bird or a night owl? Is any of the two lifestyles healthier?
10. Did you used to share a room when you were a child? What was it like?
11. Do you think what we watch, read and listen to during the day influences our dreams?
12. What do you do when you struggle to sleep?
13. Do you prefer to sleep with a duvet or a blanket? What temperature do you like the bedroom to be?
14. Do you think sleepwalking can be dangerous? What can go wrong?
15. Have you ever fallen asleep at an embarrassing moment? Describe what happened.
16. Have you ever overslept and missed something important? What was it?
17. Do you consider snoring a problem?
18. Do you think having a TV in the bedroom is a good idea? Why? Why not?
19. Do you get enough sleep? If not, what stops you from sleeping enough?
20. How many hours of sleep should a person get each day? Does everybody need the same amount of sleep?
21. Have you ever slept outside? If so, explain the situation.
22. What is the longest you have ever slept for? What made you sleep for that long?

INTERPERSONAL RELATIONS
DESCRIBE THE PICTURE AND ANSWER THE QUESTIONS

1. Do you think all children love celebrating special occasions? Why? Why not?
2. Do you like celebrating special occasions? Why? Why not?
3. Describe the best birthday party you have ever had.

Work in pairs

DISCUSS AND ANSWER THE QUESTIONS BELOW.

1. What is the biggest problem for children when their parents get divorced?
2. What are the qualities of a good listener?
3. Is empathy important? How to recognise someone lacks empathy?
4. Why is adolescence such a difficult time of life?
5. Why do you think most siblings argue?
6. Who has the biggest influence on young people? Parents? Media? School? Peers?
7. Why do people gossip? How may gossiping influence friendships?
8. Do you find telling white lies acceptable and fair?
9. Is it possible to get on well with every single person you meet?
10. Should parents check their children's social media on daily basis?

INTERPERSONAL RELATIONS
DESCRIBE THE PICTURE AND ANSWER THE QUESTIONS

1. Who do you think the women are to each other? Why are they arguing?
2. Why do people who live together argue?
3. Describe the last argument you had with someone.

Work in pairs

SPEAK FOR TWO MINUTES ABOUT THE SITUATIONS BELOW. TAKE TURNS. YOU ARE BOTH WELCOME TO ASK QUESTIONS TO EACH OTHER.

1. The last time you had a pleasant meeting with friends.
2. The last time you had an argument with someone in a shop.
3. The last time you felt embarrassed by your parents.
4. The last time you forgot about something important.
5. The last time something hilarious that happened in your life.
6. The last time you bought a gift for someone.
7. The last time you partied.
8. The last time you cooked for someone.
9. The last time you had an emergency.
10. The last time you wanted you could be a child again.

INTERPERSONAL RELATIONS
DESCRIBE THE PICTURE AND ANSWER THE QUESTIONS

1. Why do you think people get married?
2. Do you believe in marriage? Why? Why not?
3. What are some rules that should be followed for a marriage to last?
4. What would be your ideal setting for a wedding?
5. What are the most popular locations to get married in your country?

Work in pairs

READ THE FOLLOWING CHINESE PROVERBS. DISCUSS TO WHAT EXTENT YOU AGREE WITH THEM.

1. As distance tests a horse's strength, time reveals a person's character.
2. A word spoken can never be taken back.
3. Think three times before you act.
4. Good medicine tastes bitter.
5. Repay good with good.
6. Great wisdom can seem foolish.
7. Who holds hands with you, grows old with you.
8. A day's planning is done at dawn.
9. Don't miss opportunities. Time doesn't come round again.
10. All things seem difficult at the start.

INTERPERSONAL RELATIONS
DESCRIBE THE PICTURE AND ANSWER THE QUESTIONS

1. Why do you think the couple is visiting the therapist?
2. What does a perfect relationship look like?
3. Is mental health a taboo issue in your country? Why?

Work in pairs

WRITE DOWN AS MANY ADJECTIVES DESRIBING PERSONALITY AS YOU CAN THINK OF IN 2 MINUTES. DECIDE WHICH OF THESE TRAITS YOU WOULD LIKE THE FOLOWING PEOPLE TO PRESENT.

1. A friend
2. Someone you want to socialise with
3. A doctor
4. A police officer
5. A shop assistant
6. A partner
7. A teacher
8. A parent
9. A mother-in-law
10. A politician

INTERPERSONAL RELATIONS
DESCRIBE THE PICTURE AND ANSWER THE QUESTIONS.

1. What do you think it is like to be famous?
2. Has it ever been your dream? Why? Why not?
3. Do you follow any celebrities on social media? Why? Why not?
4. Do you follow fashion? Why? Why not?
5. Describe the most fashionable person you know.
6. Is appearance important to you? What aspects of it are more important than others?
7. What is your idea of beauty?
8. Describe the last time you wanted to make a good impression on someone.
9. Describe the last time you met someone who you thought seemed strange.
10. Do you think celebrities are good role models?

Work in pairs

DISCUSS AND ANSWER THE QUESTIONS BELOW.

1. How much of what you do is for yourself? How much is for other people?
2. If you see a person that looks lost on the street, do you try to help them? Why or why not?
3. Should we give money to beggars? Why? Why not?
4. Can you imagine living on the streets? What would be most uncomfortable about that situation? How would you survive?
5. Would you interfere if you saw a fight in public? What if one person was being seriously hurt?
6. Would you consider donating an organ while you are alive, like a kidney or a lung?
7. Do you trust charitable organizations? Which organizations are most trustworthy?

WORK
DESCRIBE THE PICTURE AND ANSWER THE QUESTIONS

1. How would you describe the atmosphere in the office in the picture?
2. What are some important rules concerning team work?
3. Which jobs do you think will disappear in the future?
4. Which jobs do you think will be more popular in the future?
5. What is your dream job and why?
6. If you were to open your own business what would it be and why?
7. What are some qualities of a good employee?

Situational English

YOU HAVE FOUND AN INTERESTING JOB OFFER IN THE LOCAL JOB CENTRE. RING THE OFFICE TO LEARN MORE.

- Give the reason for your call.
- Learn what requirements there are for applicants to get the job.
- Learn more about working hours, wages, type of contract, etc.
- Get to know what documents you need and how you should apply for the job.

Situational English

YOU WORK AS A SECRETARY IN A LANGUAGE SCHOOL. ACT OUT A PHONE CALL WITH A PROSPECTIVE STUDENT

- Ask about basic personal details.
- Learn which type of course the caller is interested in.
- Allocate the caller to a particular group, give information about payments and timetable.
- Ask if the caller agrees to the terms and wants to enroll to classes.

WORK
DESCRIBE THE PICTURE AND ANSWER THE QUESTIONS

1. What examples of observing health and safety measures can you see in the picture? Do you think they are enough to ensure safety in the construction site?
2. Do you think construction work can be dangerous? Give some examples in support of your opinion.
3. Which jobs do you think are severely underpaid and which are overpaid? Why do you think that is?
4. Which jobs do you think are among the most dangerous in the world?
5. Are any jobs more suitable for men or women than others? Why?
6. Which job would you never agree to do and why?
7. What are some qualities of a good team leader?

Situational English

YOU HAVE FALLEN ILL. RING YOUR MANAGER AND INFORM HIM OR HER YOU NEED A COUPLE OF DAYS OFF.

- Give the reason for your call.
- Inform the manager what your symptoms are and how long do you think you will be off.
- Ask what documents do you need to fill in.

Situational English

THERE HAS BEEN AN ACCIDENT AT YOUR WORKPLACE. YOU NEED TO CALL AN AMBULANCE.

- Introduce yourself and give personal details of the injured co-worker.
- Describe your co-worker's condition.
- Describe the circumstances of the event.
- Listen for further instructions and react accordingly.

WORK
DESCRIBE THE PICTURES AND ANSWER THE QUESTIONS

1. What are some factors that make a job tiring, stressful and unsatisfactory?
2. What are the qualities of a good and a bad boss?
3. What can be done to improve conditions at work?
4. What do you do to reduce stress?
5. What would you do if you had a difficult manager or a co-worker?

Additional questions:
1. Where would you start to look for a job?
2. Would you prefer to work in a large or a small company? Why?
3. Are you good at working under pressure? Share some examples.
4. Would you like to be in charge of other people? Why? Why not?
5. Do you think atmosphere at work influences productivity? Why? Why not?
6. What are some good and bad sides of working from home?
7. What would make you quit a job instantly?
8. Could you do a very well-paid job that you do not enjoy? Why? Why not?

WORK
DESCRIBE THE PICTURE AND ANSWER THE QUESTIONS

1. Do you think the woman finds her job satisfactory?
2. What are the qualities of a good sales person?
3. Have ever considered doing a part-time or a holiday job? Why? Why not?
4. What would you or did you spend your first salary on?

Work in pairs

PERSON "A" CHOOSES A JOB OR A PROFESSION. PERSON "B" USES THE QUESTIONS BELOW TO INTERVIEW PERSON "A". THEN YOU SWAP.

- Why did you choose to do this job?
- What do you find the most and the least enjoyable about this job?
- Do you think your job is important to society? What makes you say that?
- Is your job ever stressful? In what ways?
- Describe the greatest moment in your career.
- Describe your first day at work.
- What are your strong points that make you good at what you are doing?

WORK
DESCRIBE THE PICTURE AND ANSWER THE QUESTIONS

1. Do you think the woman finds her job satisfactory?
2. Do you think being a fashion designer is an easy job? What makes you think so?
3. What job would be your passion?

Work in pairs

PERSON "A" SPEAKS FOR A MINUTE ON A GIVEN TOPIC. PERSON "B" ASKS WH-QUESTIONS TO LEARN MORE DETAILS. THEN YOU SWAP.

Talk about:

- Someone whose business is doing very well.
- Someone who has decided to set up an online business.
- Someone who has been unemployed.
- Someone who got fired.
- Someone who has a good salary but does not get on well with their boss.
- Someone who works really hard and has to do overtime.
- Someone who has been promoted recently.
- Someone who is self-employed.
- Someone you would like to work with.
- Someone who is very creative at work.

WORK
DESCRIBE THE PICTURE AND ANSWER THE QUESTIONS

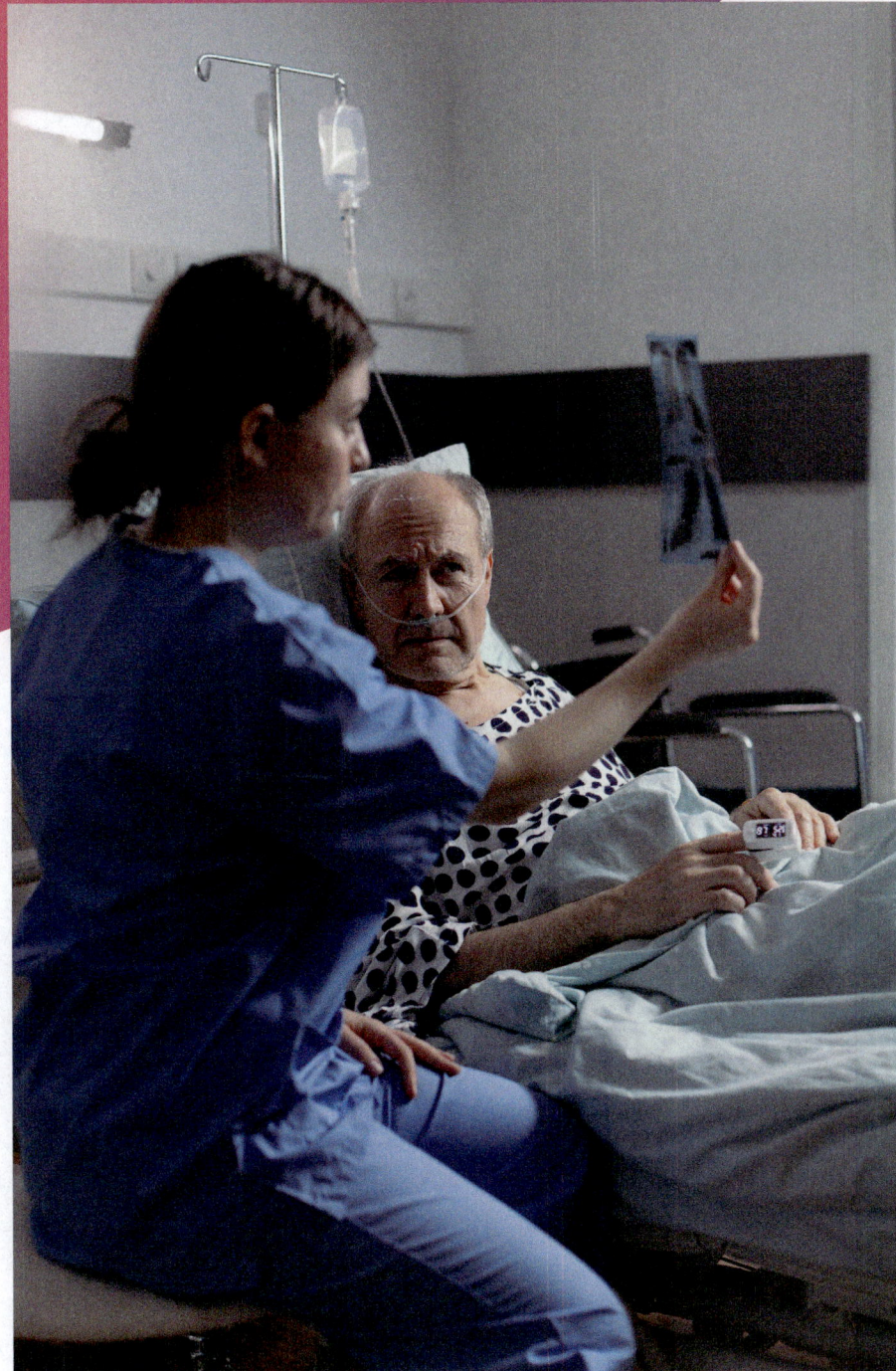

1. Do you think the specialist finds her work easy or difficult?
2. What are some qualities of a good doctor, nurse or other medical specialist?
3. How would you describe medical care system in your country?
4. Has the pandemic increased or decreased the level of trust people have towards medical specialists?
5. What can be done to improve health care conditions?
6. Would you like to work as a doctor or a nurse? Why? Why not?
7. Why do you think people pick medical careers nowadays?
8. Describe the last time you or someone you know went to hospital.
9. Would you like to work abroad? Why? Why not?

Additional questions:
1. Do you think it is necessary to have higher education to find a good job? Why do you think so?
2. Which professions are definitely not for you? Why?
3. It is better to spend your money in your lifetime or leave an inheritance to your family?.
4. Do you think it is a good idea to drop out of school and start working at an early age? Why? Why not?

WORK
DESCRIBE THE PICTURES AND ANSWER THE QUESTIONS

1. What are the main symptoms of work burnout?
2. What are the most serious consequences of prolonged stress?
3. Who would you ask for help were you experiencing problems at work?

Additional questions:
1. What is more important in planning a career: following your passion or considering career prospects?
2. How do you understand the notion of living to work rather than working to live?
3. How do you understand job satisfaction?.
4. Would you prefer to have one job throughout your entire life or change professions from time to time? What are the advantages and disadvantages of both situations?

WORK
DESCRIBE THE PICTURES AND ANSWER THE QUESTIONS

1. What qualities a person must have to be a good engineer?
2. What are some possible injuries one might suffer in a workplace like this?

1. Do you think the woman in the picture is satisfied with her job? Why?
2. Which of the two jobs would you prefer to do and why?

WORK
DESCRIBE THE PICTURES AND ANSWER THE QUESTIONS

1. What are some pros and cons of working with machinery?
2. Do you think you would be a good technician?

1. Do you think one needs to have green fingers to work with plants?
2. Which of the two jobs would you prefer to do and why?
3. What agricultural products are grown in your country?

MEDICINE AND HEALTH
DESCRIBE THE PICTURES AND ANSWER THE QUESTIONS

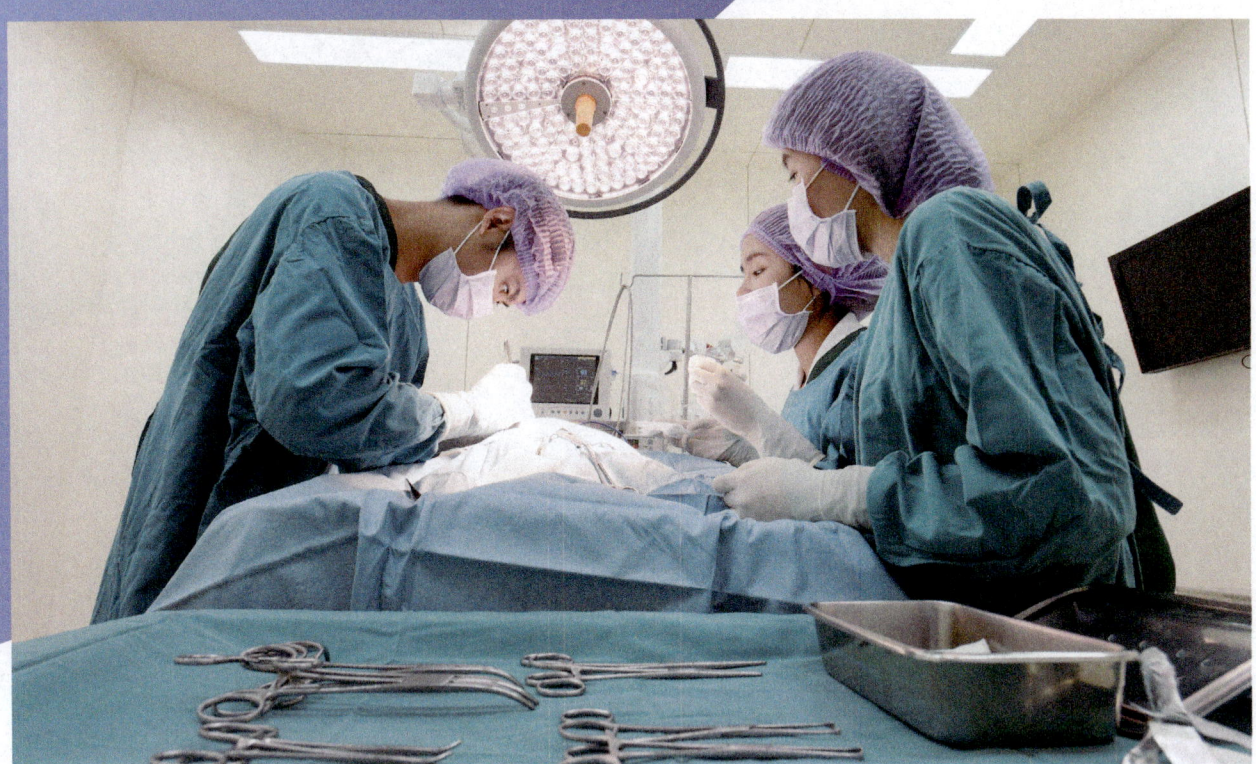

1. What are some qualities of a good surgeon?
2. Do you think being a doctor is an easy job? Why? Why not?

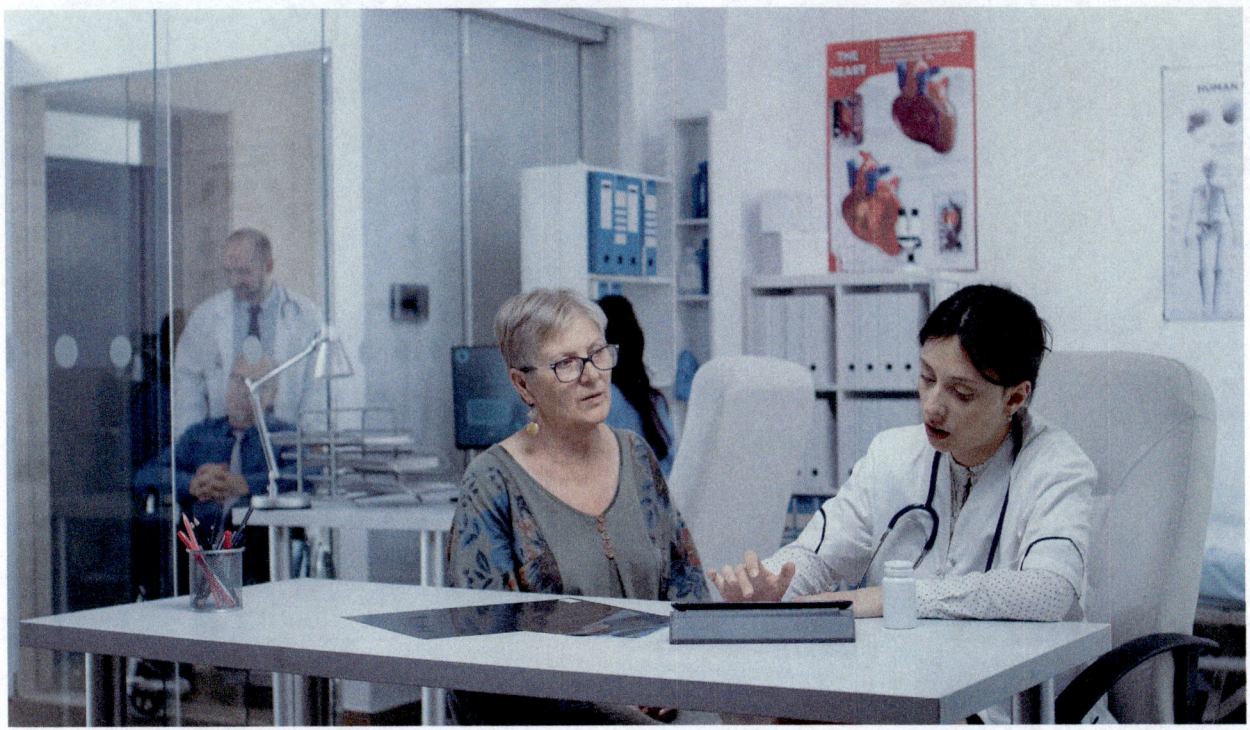

1. Do you think the woman in the picture is enjoying her job? Why? Why not?
2. What are some most common diseases elderly people suffer from and why?
3. How would you describe a healthy lifestyle?

MEDICINE AND HEALTH
DESCRIBE THE PICTURES AND ANSWER THE QUESTIONS

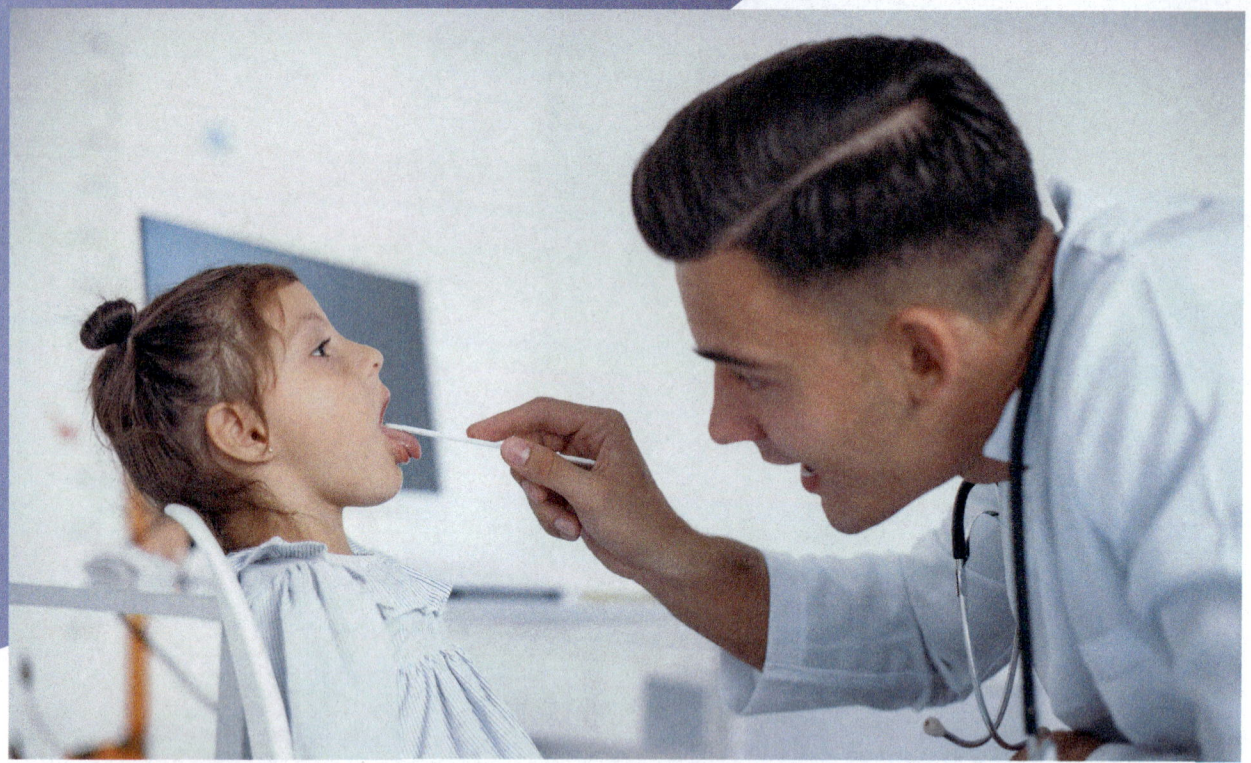

1. Do you think the man is a good doctor?
2. What are the main reasons that make children afraid of medical specialists?

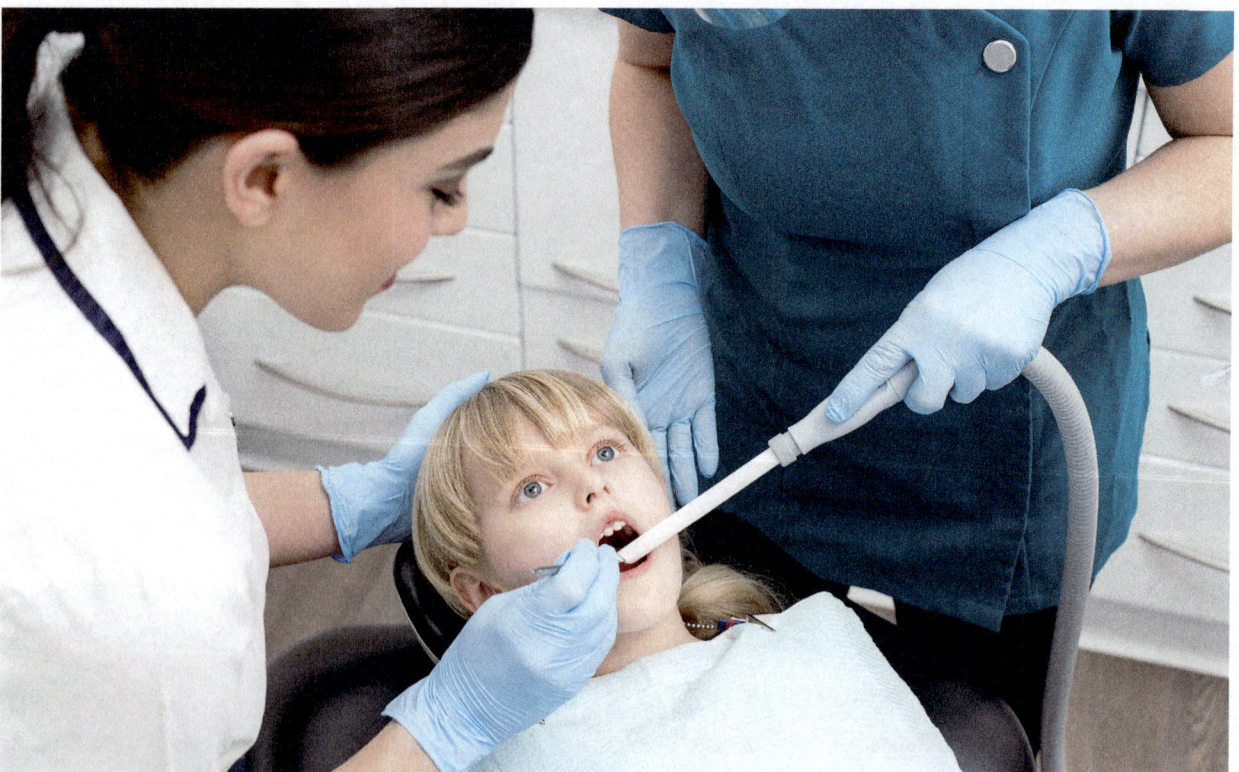

1. What do you think the child is feeling?
2. Are you scared of going to the dentist? Elaborate on that.

24

MEDICINE AND HEALTH
DESCRIBE THE PICTURE AND ANSWER THE QUESTIONS

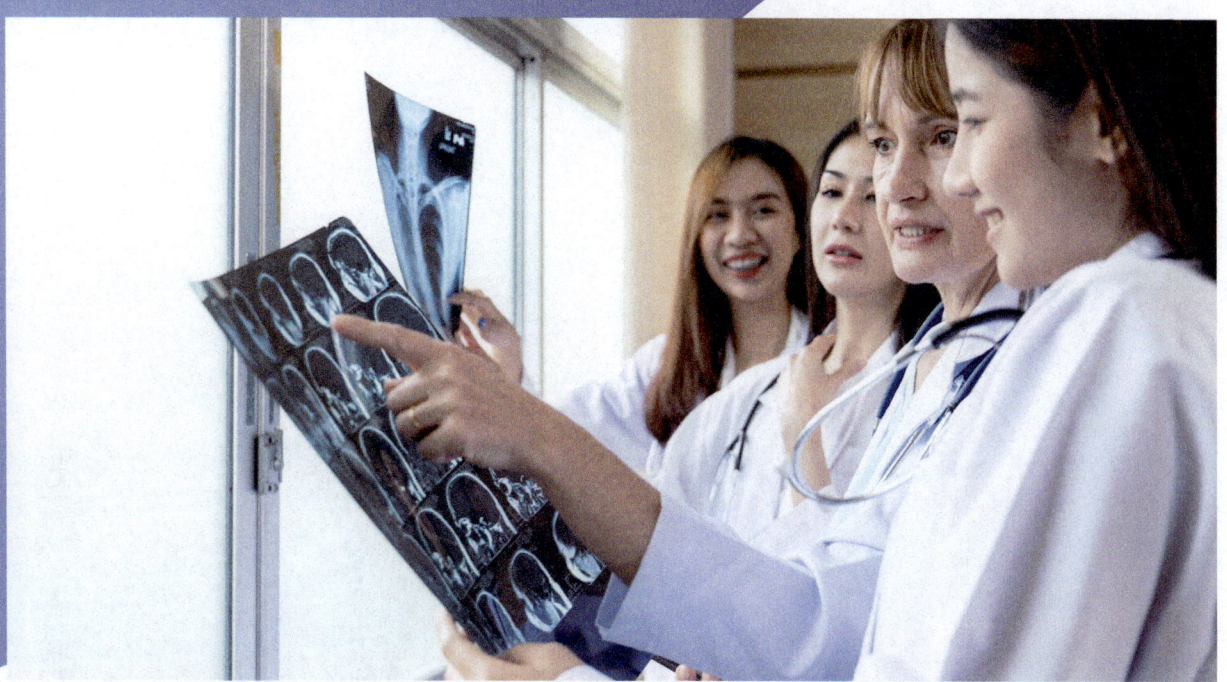

1. Do you think studying medicine is difficult? What makes you think so?
2. Have ever considered becoming a doctor? Why or why not?

Do you agree with the sentences? Discuss with a partner.
1. Most people do not care how long they will live.
2. Most people do not care what they eat.
3. Most people know drugs are dangerous.
4. People eat fast food because it is cheap and accessible everywhere.
5. Smoking should be banned in all public places.
6. Social media and fashion industry are to be blamed for epidemic of food disorders like anorexia and bulimia.
7. Most people have little knowledge concerning the danger of sexually transmitted diseases.
8. Most people tend to search for solutions online rather than visit a specialist.
9. Most people do not attend regular heath checks.
10. Most people prefer to take tablets and see quick results rather than change the lifestyle and see long-term improvement that takes some effort.
11. Most people do not trust doctors nowadays.
12. Most young people will not live as long as their parents.
13. Some diseases could be stopped but it is not profitable to do so.
14. People who live in rural areas are much healthier than those who live in big cities.
15. Vegetarian diet is the healthiest diet in the world.

MEDICINE AND HEALTH
DESCRIBE THE PICTURE AND ANSWER THE QUESTIONS

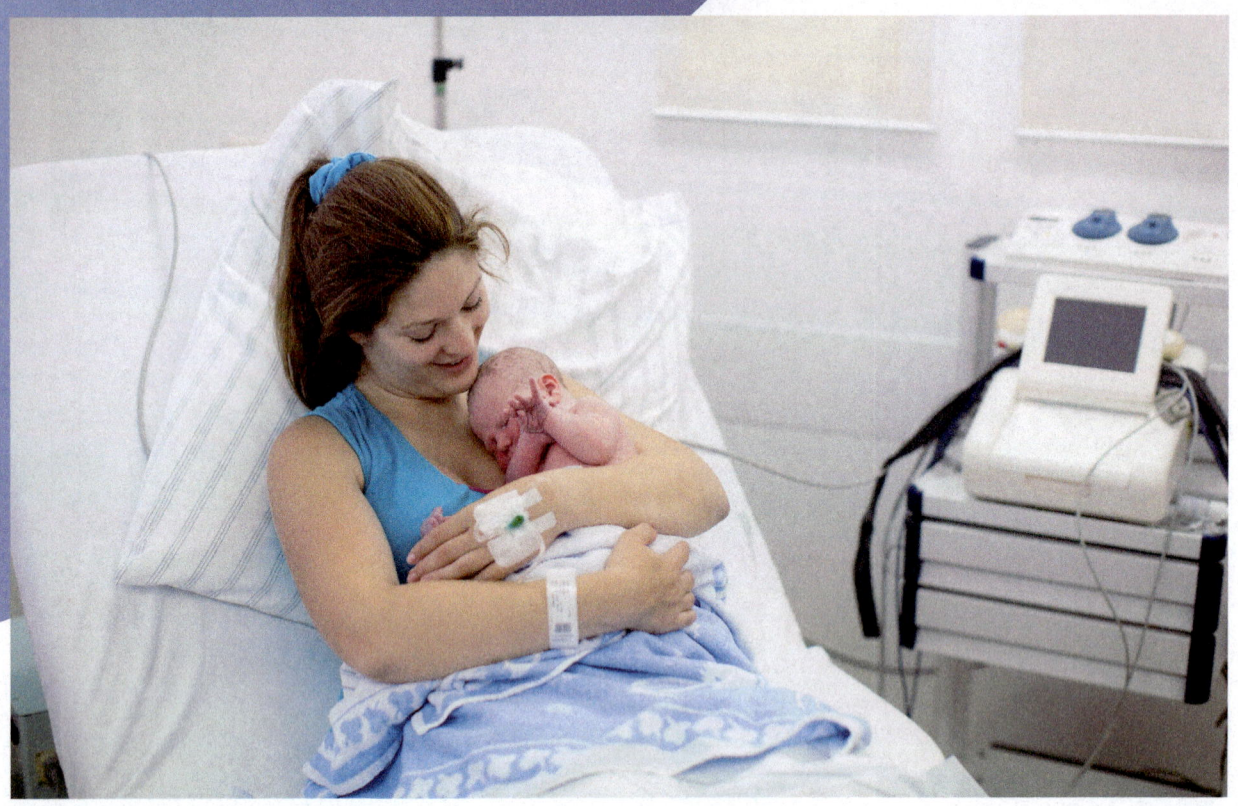

1. How do you think the woman feels?
2. Do you have or do you want to have children? Why or why not?

PERSON "A" SPEAKS FOR A MINUTE ON A GIVEN TOPIC. PERSON "B" ASKS WH-QUESTIONS TO LEARN MORE DETAILS. THEN YOU SWAP.

Talk about:
- Someone who has been hospitalised recently.
- Someone who has broken a limb recently.
- Someone who has been involved in a car accident.
- Someone who has given birth to a child.
- Someone who studies medicine.
- Someone who works at a local doctor's surgery.
- Someone who works at a hospital.
- Someone who is scared of the dentist.
- Someone who has poor eyesight.
- Someone who has high blood pressure.
- Someone who should take better care of themselves.
- Someone who should quit smoking.
- Someone who is very fit.
- Someone who takes care of you when you are sick.

MEDICINE AND HEALTH
DESCRIBE THE PICTURE AND ANSWER THE QUESTIONS

1. How do you think the woman feels and why?
2. What three tips would you give someone who has caught a cold?
3. What do you think is important when it comes to establishing a proper diagnosis?

Work in pairs

DO YOU KNOW WHAT TO DO IF...

- Someone is choking.
- Someone has burnt their skin.
- Someone has cut themselves and is bleeding heavily.
- Someone is having a nosebleed.
- Someone has collapsed on the ground.
- Someone has very high temperature.
- Someone has been stung by a wasp and has an allergic reaction.
- Someone has very bad sunburn.
- Someone struggles to sleep.
- Someone often gets colds.
- Someone has fallen and broken their leg.
- Someone has lost consciousness.

MEDICINE AND HEALTH
DESCRIBE THE PICTURE AND ANSWER THE QUESTIONS

1. What do you think has happened to the patient?
2. Describe a situation when you or someone you know felt very stressed.
3. What are the best ways of keeping your body and mind healthy?

Do you agree with the sentences?

1. Most young people are stressed out because they want to come up to their parents' expectations.
2. Permanent stress affects the mind more than the body.
3. Young generation does not know how to deal with stress.
4. Having a positive attitude helps to prevent mental breakdowns.
5. Dreams can tell us a lot about our health.
6. Natural methods are the best when it comes to fighting with a common cold.
7. Young people do not care about their lifestyle.
8. Money cannot buy health.
9. Healthcare would work better if it was private.
10. Treatment of some diseases should be compulsory even if it means breaking human rights of an individual.

MEDICINE AND HEALTH
DESCRIBE THE PICTURE AND ANSWER THE QUESTIONS

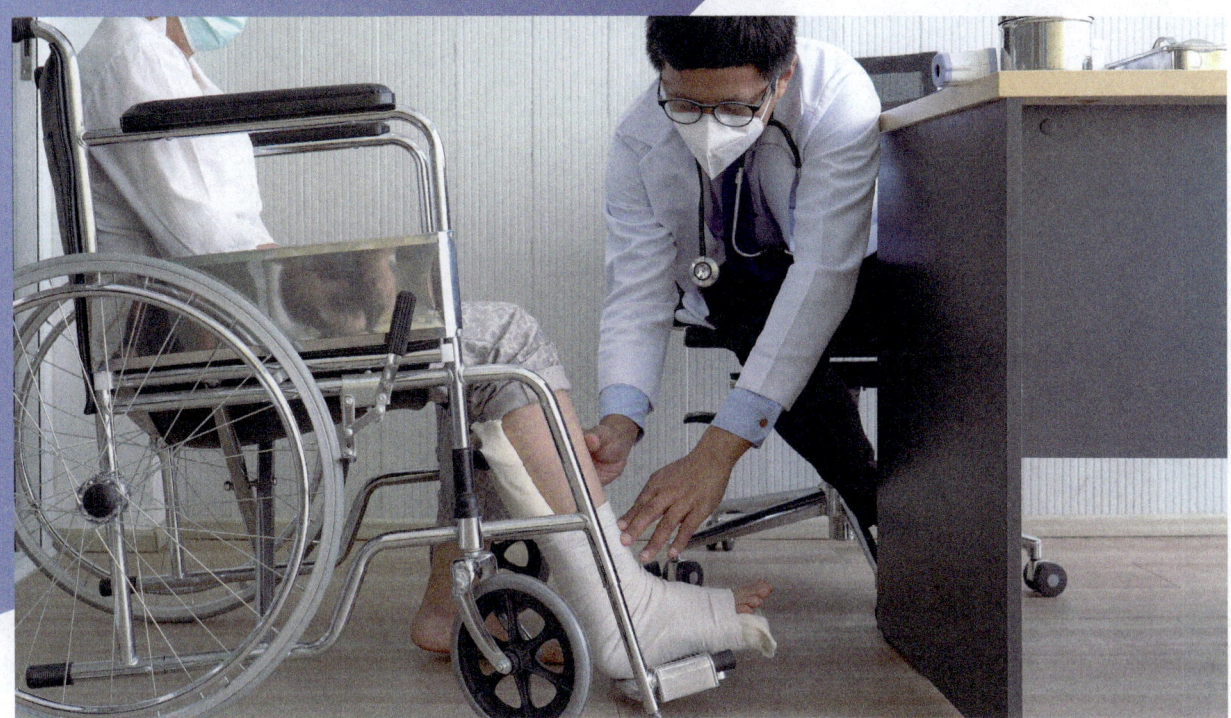

1. What do you think has happened to the patient?
2. In what situations do people tend to break they limbs?
3. Describe a situation when you or someone you know needed to wear a plaster cast.

Situational English

YOU WORK AS A RECEPTIONIST AT A DOCTOR'S SURGERY. YOU ARE TALKING TO A PATIENT WHO WOULD LIKE TO HAVE AN APPOINTMENT WITH A DOCTOR WHO IS CURRENTLY ON A SICK LEAVE.

- Inform the patient why the appointment cannot take place.
- Offer an appointment with a different specialist or an appointment at a different date.
- Inform the patient what documents are necessary for the appointment.
- Apologise for the inconvenience.

Situational English

YOU WERE TO VISIT YOUR FAMILY IN A DIFFERENT COUNTRY. UNFORTUNATELY YOU HAVE BROKEN YOUR LEG. RING THE FAMILY.

- Apologise for the unexpected change of plans.
- Explain why you cannot visit them.
- Describe how you broke your leg.
- Describe who helped you at the scene and how.
- Tell them how you are going to wear the plaster cast.
- Ask if you can visit them some other time.
- Ask how they are doing.

MEDICINE AND HEALTH
DESCRIBE THE PICTURES AND ANSWER THE QUESTIONS

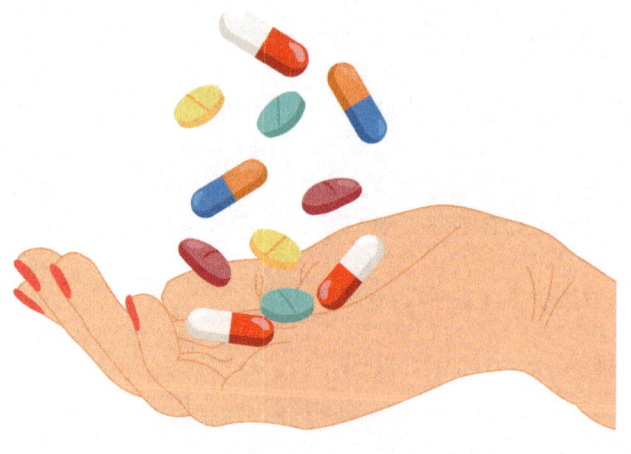

1. What do you think is the difference between traditional and alternative medicine? Do you have any preferences?
2. Do you know anyone who regularly uses a natural medicine specialist? What is your opinion on that?
3. How would you describe your physical health?

FOOD
DESCRIBE THE PICTURE AND ANSWER THE QUESTIONS

1. Who do you think the people in the picture are to each other? What makes you think so?
2. Do you think it is important to eat healthy food?
3. Do you prefer to cook your own food or to order it from outside?

Can you think of...?

1. Three red fruit, three green fruit and three yellow fruit.
2. Five kinds of food people are often allergic to.
3. Three kinds of food people tend to get addicted to.
4. Seven vegetables that you can put in a salad.
5. Five vegetables that many children do not like.
6. Five containers you can buy food in.
7. Six things people usually have for breakfast.
8. Five things you eat when you feel down.
9. Three kinds of food you could not live without.
10. Five kinds of food you do not like.

FOOD
DESCRIBE THE PICTURE AND ANSWER THE QUESTIONS

1. Is there anything the woman in the photo could do to improve her diet?
2. Why do you think people eat fast food?
3. What food do you usually eat when you are in a hurry?

Work in pairs

DISCUSS AND DECIDE UPON ANSWERS TO THE QUESTIONS:

- What kind of food is recommended before an exam?
- What kind of food should be eaten for an evening meal?
- How often do you think it is healthy to eat sweets?
- Are men better cooks than women?
- Should both boys and girls learn to cook?
- Do cheap restaurants serve bad food?
- Is all fast food unhealthy?
- Is there any cuisine which is more unique than others?
- What is more important: what you eat or with whom you share a meal?
- Does the younger generation eat out more often than their parents?

FOOD
DESCRIBE THE PICTURE AND ANSWER THE QUESTIONS

1. Why do you think the woman is recording herself cooking?
2. What do you think a balanced diet looks like?
3. What is the role of social media in what people eat?

Work in pairs

ASK EACH OTHER QUESTIONS TO FILL IN THE PERSONAL FOOD QUESTIONNAIRE.

- How often do you eat out?
- What is your favourite food?
- What do you usually have for breakfast?
- Are you a good cook?
- Do you need to buy any food today?
- Are you planning to cook anything today?
- What is your specialty?
- What is your favourite cuisine?
- How would you describe the diet in your country?
- Are you trying to cut down on any food at the moment?
- Who taught you to cook?
- Is there any food that brings back memories of your mother or grandmother?

FOOD

DESCRIBE THE PICTURE AND ANSWER THE QUESTIONS

1. Who do you think the people in the picture are?
2. What is the recipe for your favourite cake?
3. Are you a fussy eater?

Work in pairs

IMAGINE YOU OWN A RESTAURANT. TOGETHER WITH A PARTNER DECIDE UPON ITS NAME AND ITS PROFILE. ANSWER THE FOLLOWING QUESTIONS.

- What is the name of your restaurant?
- Where is it located?
- What food do you serve?
- How many people do you employ?
- Do you deliver food?
- What are the most important things in a restaurant? Is it service, atmosphere?
- What do you think are the best and the worst things about running a restaurant?
- How do you deal with difficult customers?
- What marketing strategies do you use to draw customers?

FOOD
DESCRIBE THE PICTURES AND ANSWER THE QUESTIONS

1. What makes people enjoy barbecuing?
2. Do you prefer to eat alone or in company? Why?
3. Do you like similar outings? Why? Why not?

Which of the three places would you choose for a romantic dinner and why?

FOOD

DESCRIBE THE PICTURE AND ANSWER THE QUESTIONS

1. Do you think the child often eats like that?
2. What could she do to improve her eating habits?
3. Why is it unhealthy to eat in front of a TV or a screen?

Situational English

YOU ARE CALLING YOUR FRIEND TO INVITE HIM OR HER FOR A DINNER.

- Inform the friend when and where you want to meet.
- Tell them why you want to meet.
- Tell them if there is going to be anyone else.
- Tell them what type of food the restaurant serves.

Situational English

YOU ARE ON A TRIP TO SOME TROPICAL COUNTRY. UNFORTUNATELY YOU GOT AN AWFUL FOOD POISONING. YOU ARE CALLING YOUR GP TO ASK FOR HELP.

- Introduce yourself.
- Say why you are calling and what your symptoms are.
- Say what you ate and where.
- Ask for advice.

FOOD

DESCRIBE THE PICTURE AND ANSWER THE QUESTIONS

1. Do you think the kids are enjoying cooking?
2. Should children be taught to cook? At what age?
3. Can you cook? When did you learn?

Do you agree?

- School dinners should be funded by the government.
- Good food improves our concentration.
- Good food makes us live longer.
- All cereals are good for health.
- We should not eat red meat.
- The number of restaurants increases every year.
- More and more people have food allergies.
- Chocolate can never be bad for us.
- Eating meals together helps to strengthen bonds.
- Making your own food is cheaper than eating out.
- Schools should be able to sell sweets and crisps. Kids should have a choice what they eat rather than be forced to eat what their parents eat.

TRAVEL AND TOURISM

DESCRIBE THE PICTURE AND ANSWER THE QUESTIONS

1. Do you think the women are enjoying their vacation?
2. Is it safe to travel anywhere in the world?
3. Are there any places you would like to visit and places you would prefer to avoid? Why?

Would you prefer?

- going abroad or travelling around your own country
- going by car, train or plane
- visiting countries similar to yours or trying something completely new
- going to the beach or going to the city
- staying in an expensive hotel or sleeping in a tent
- sunbathing or sightseeing
- going somewhere hot or cold
- going with people or going alone
- going with friends or with family
- spending money on travelling or saving it for something else

TRAVEL AND TOURISM

DESCRIBE THE PICTURES AND ANSWER THE QUESTIONS

1. Which of the three vacation types would you like to take and why?
2. Describe pros and cons of each type of holiday making in terms of money, safety, adventure, etc.
3. What do you take into consideration while planning a holiday?
4. Describe the best and the worst holiday you have ever had.

Work in pairs
FORM QUESTIONS AND INTERVIEW EACH OTHER
- Where/go/holidays
- Who/go/with
- Where/stay
- How long/stay
- What/weather like
- What/ the food like
- Enjoy/the holiday
- What/ do during the holiday
- What/do at night
- Have any problems

TRAVEL AND TOURISM

DESCRIBE THE PICTURE AND ANSWER THE QUESTIONS

1. What do you think the woman does for a living?
2. Describe the last time you or someone you know were travelling by plane.
3. Which means of transport do you think is the safest?

Work in pairs

DISCUSS THE FOLLOWING SENTENCES AND DECIDE TO WHAT EXTENT YOU AGREE

- Travelling by plane is always the quickest way.
- Driving is more boring than going by train.
- Women drive more carefully than men.
- Driving on the left is safer than driving on the right.
- Driving a large car is safer than driving a small car.
- Cycling is more dangerous than riding a motor bike.
- It is easier to learn to drive than to learn to ride a horse.
- Being stuck in a traffic jam is more boring than waiting at the airport.
- Slow drivers cause more accidents than fast drivers.
- People who drink and drive should lose their driving licence for life.
- Speed cameras help to decrease the amount of accidents.
- Drivers who are over 70 should have their driving licence endorsed.
- The speed limit on motorways should be higher.
- Cyclists should have to wear helmets and special fluorescent vests.
- The minimum age for riding a motorbike should be 26.

TRAVEL AND TOURISM

DESCRIBE WHERE THE CHILDREN ARE IN REFERENCE TO OTHER OBJECTS. USE PREPOSITIONS OF PLACE (BEHIND, IN FRONT, IN THE MIDDLE, ETC.)

Work in pairs

DECIDE WHICH OF THESE ACTIVITIES ARE DANGEROUS WHEN YOU ARE DRIVING A CAR AND WHY.

1. **Texting**
2. **Smoking**
3. **Eating and drinking**
4. **Talking on the phone while holding it**
5. **Talking on the phone using a hands free set**
6. **Listening to loud music**
7. **Doing makeup**
8. **Setting a satnav**

TRAVEL AND TOURISM

WORK IN PAIRS. DO NOT SHOW THE PICTURES TO EACH OTHER BEFORE YOU FINISH THE EXERCISE. PERSON "A" DESCRIBES PICTURE "A" SO THAT PERSON "B" CAN DRAW IT. THEN PERSON "B" DESCRIBES PICTURE "B" AND PERSON "A" DRAWS IT.

TRAVEL AND TOURISM

PLAY HIDE AND SEEK IN PAIRS. DECIDE WHERE IS YOUR STARTING POINT. PERSON "A" CHOOSES A PLACE TO HIDE AND DESCRIBES HOW TO GET THERE. PERSON "B" GUESSES THE HIDING SPOT. THEN YOU SWAP.

Situational English

YOU ARE ON A TRIP TO EUROPE. CALL YOUR FRIEND.

- Inform them where you are right now.
- Tell them what have you been doing so far.
- Tell them who have you met.
- Describe the weather.
- Tell them what have you enjoyed the most so far.
- Tell them when are you planning to come back.
- Tell them you miss them.

Situational English

YOU ARE ON A TRIP TO LONDON. YOU GOT LOST. TALK TO A PERSON IN THE STREET.

- Ask the person if they speak English.
- Ask if they are local.
- Say you got lost and ask where you are.
- Say where you want to go.
- Ask for directions.
- Thank for their help.

TRAVEL AND TOURISM

DESCRIBE THE PICTURE AND ANSWER THE QUESTIONS

1. Why do you think they got lost?
2. Describe the last time you or someone you know got lost. How did you feel? Who helped you? How did it end?
3. When you travel what tourist attractions do you like visiting?

Work in pairs

PERSON "A" DESCRIBES THE LAST TIME SOMETHING HAPPENED.
PERSON "B" ASKS WH-QUESTIONS TO LEARN MORE. THEN YOU SWAP.

1. **Have an accident**
2. **The car/ break down**
3. **Run out of petrol**
4. **The plane/ late**
5. **Feel sick**
6. **Lose money**
7. **Long tiring journey**
8. **Get lost**
9. **Forget passport**
10. **Luggage/ go missing**

TRAVEL AND TOURISM

DESCRIBE THE PICTURES AND ANSWER THE QUESTIONS

1. Which picture shows your dream holiday and why?
2. Which place would you not want to visit and why?
3. What can go wrong while visiting any of these places?

Work in pairs

DECIDE WHAT THE PROS AND CONS OF THE FOLLOWING TYPES OF HOLIDAYS ARE. WHICH OF THESE WOULD YOU LIKE TO TAKE?

1. A safari
2. A winter holiday
3. All-inclusive holiday
4. A cruise
5. A beach holiday
6. An adventure holiday

TRAVEL AND TOURISM

DESCRIBE THE PICTURE AND ANSWER THE QUESTIONS

1. Do you think such markets add value to the community? Why? Why not?
2. What can be sold at a town market?
3. Do you like visiting such places? Why? Why not?

Work in pairs

DISCUSS THE FOLLOWING SENTENCES AND DECIDE TO WHAT EXTENT YOU AGREE WITH THEM.

- People like holidays that provide them with some kind of thrill.
- Hitchhiking can be dangerous.
- It is fun to travel to deserted places.
- Weather can spoil a holiday easily.
- Travelling on your own is the best way to relax.
- Mixing with the locals when on holiday helps you get to know the culture better.
- Visiting historical places is fun for young people.

TRAVEL AND TOURISM

DESCRIBE THE PICTURE AND ANSWER THE QUESTIONS

1. Do you think the man's work is easy or difficult? What makes you say so?
2. Have you ever been to a similar place? Describe it.
3. Do you like visiting such places? Why? Why not?

Work in pairs

DISCUSS AND ANSWER THE FOLLOWING QUESTIONS.

- What is the most romantic city in the world?
- What is the cleanest country in the world?
- What is the dirtiest city in your country?
- Which city in your country has the oldest architecture?
- Where have you met the friendliest people?
- What is the most beautiful city you have ever been to?
- What is the most expensive thing you have even bought on holiday?
- What is your country famous for?
- What is the most exciting thing you have ever done on holiday?
- What is the most interesting thing you have ever learnt on holiday?
- What is the most frightening thing that has ever happened to you on holiday?

TRAVEL AND TOURISM

DESCRIBE THE PICTURES AND ANSWER THE QUESTIONS

1. Imagine you could travel around the world using only one of the means of transport shown in the pictures above. Which one would you choose?
2. What are the advantages and disadvantages of using each means of transport?
3. How do you think people will travel in the future?
4. What is the best means of transport to use in the city?
5. How has the way people travel changed over the years?

HOUSE AND HOME

DESCRIBE THE PICTURES AND ANSWER THE QUESTIONS

1. Discuss advantages and disadvantages of living in every house shown in the pictures.
2. Which one would you prefer to live in and why?
3. Describe the house you live in now.
4. Who do you live with? Do you get on well?

Work in pairs

DISCUSS THE FOLLOWING SENTENCES AND DECIDE TO WHAT EXTENT YOU BOTH AGREE.

- We will soon be able to control our houses when we are not there.
- It is better to live far from civilisation rather than to live in a big city.
- It is better to live alone than to live with a family.
- Youngsters should move out when they reach adulthood.
- Old fashioned interiors are cosier than modern ones.
- There are certain household chores that only women should be doing.
- Teenagers should be paid for doing household chores.

HOUSE AND HOME

DESCRIBE THE PICTURES AND ANSWER THE QUESTIONS

1. Which living room design appeals to you the most and why?
2. What are the advantages and disadvantages of living alone and living with a family?
3. Describe your living room.

Work in pairs

WHAT IS THE DIFFERENCE BETWEEN…?

1. A balcony and a terrace
2. A roof and a ceiling
3. A village and a town
4. A town and a city
5. A chimney and a fireplace
6. The ground floor and the first floor
7. The outskirts and the suburbs
8. A bungalow and a detached house
9. A detached house and a terraced house
10. A studio flat and a flat

HOUSE AND HOME

DESCRIBE THE PICTURE AND ANSWER THE QUESTIONS

1. Why do you think the couple is moving houses?
2. If you could live anywhere in the world where would it be and why?
3. Why do you think removals are stressful.

Work in pairs

PERSON "A" HAS A PROPERTY TO RENT. PERSON "B" IS LOOKING FOR A PLACE TO RENT. CREATE A DIALOGUE WHERE PERSON "B" LEARNS THE DETAILS CONCERNING THE PROPERTY. THEN SWAP.

1. Proximity/ public transport facilities
2. Cost/ rent
3. Rent/ include bills
4. Fully furnished
5. When/ move into
6. How long/ contract
7. Neighbourhood
8. Pets/ allowed

HOUSE AND HOME

DESCRIBE THE PICTURE AND ANSWER THE QUESTIONS

1. What do young people need to do to buy a house these days?
2. What are some risks of taking a mortgage?
3. Do you think young people's life is easier or more difficult compared to their parents' life when they were young? What makes you think so?

Work in pairs

IMAGINE THERE ARE FOUR PEOPLE LIVING IN A HOUSE. A MOTHER, A FATHER, A TEENAGE DAUGHTER AND A TEENAGE SON. DISCUSS AND DECIDE WHO SHOULD BE RESPONSIBLE FOR DOING WHICH HOUSEHOLD CHORES AND WHY.

1. Cooking
2. Cleaning the kitchen
3. Cleaning the toilet
4. Taking the rubbish out
5. Mowing the lawn
6. Repairing broken equipment
7. Watering the plants
8. Doing food shopping
9. Ironing
10. Loading the dishwasher

HOUSE AND HOME

DESCRIBE THE PICTURE AND ANSWER THE QUESTIONS

1. Why do you think the room is so messy?
2. What is the messiest room in your place? Describe it.
3. What would you throw away if you had to move to a smaller place?
4. What is the division of chores in your household?

Work in pairs

ASK EACH OTHER THE FOLLOWING QUESTIONS.

1. How easy or difficult would it be for you to share a room or a flat with a stranger? Why?
2. What are the qualities of a good flatmate? Would you make a good flatmate? Why?
3. Have you or anyone you know ever shared a room? Describe the experience.
4. What questions should you ask to a landlord when you are looking for a flat?
5. What size property do you need to feel comfortable? Why?

HOUSE AND HOME

DESCRIBE THE PICTURES AND ANSWER THE QUESTIONS

1. How do you think the man is feeling and why?
2. Do you think it is better to do re-decoration on your own or to hire a specialists? What are the pros and cons of both options?
3. Describe the last time you or someone you know had your house re-decorated.
4. If you could afford any re-decoration what would you like to change in your house or flat?

1. Do you think this is a hotel room or a private bedroom? What makes you think so?
2. Would you like your bedroom to look like that? Why? Why not?
3. What do you take into consideration when you are looking for a hotel?

HOUSE AND HOME

WORK IN PAIRS. PERSON "A" DESCRIBES THE PICTURE SO THAT PERSON "B" CAN FIND 10 DIFFERENCES.

1. Who do you think lives in this room?
2. Can you guess the person's age, interests or habits?
3. Is it possible to feel good in a messy room?
4. If you could change one thing only in your room what would it be?

HOUSE AND HOME

WORK IN PAIRS. PERSON "B" DESCRIBES THE PICTURE SO THAT PERSON "A" CAN FIND 6 DIFFERENCES.

SPORTS

DESCRIBE THE PICTURE AND ANSWER THE QUESTIONS

1. Do you think using animals for sports is cruel? Why? Why not?
2. What other sports do you know that involve animals? Do you like watching or doing them?

Work in pairs

ASK EACH OTHER THE FOLLOWING QUESTIONS.

1. Do you do any sports or exercise? Do you enjoy it? Why? Why not?
2. Which sports do you think are the most boring and why?
3. Are there any sports that do not make any sense in your opinion?
4. Which sports do you think are the most exciting to watch?
5. What is the most exciting sporting event you have ever seen? Describe it.
6. Do you think there is too much football on TV?
7. What sports do you hate watching on TV and why?
8. Do you think PE should be optional or compulsory at school?
9. Do you prefer doing sport or watching sport?
10. Have you or anyone you know ever won any trophy? Describe it.
11. Do you know any superstitions connected with sport?
12. What is your opinion about betting on sports?

SPORTS

DESCRIBE THE PICTURE AND ANSWER THE QUESTIONS

1. What game do you think the people are watching? What makes you think so?
2. Do you like watching sports? Who do you support?
3. What do you think makes spectators misbehave at stadiums?

Work in pairs

TELL YOUR PARTNER SOME ANECDOTES. CHOOSE TWO OF THE TOPICS BELOW.

1. A time when you had an accident or got a sports injury. What happened? How did it happen? When and where was it? Did you get badly hurt? How long did it take you to recover?
2. An exciting sports event you saw. What was it? Who was playing? When and where did the game take place? What happened? Why was it exciting?
3. A time when you got lost. Where were you going? Why did you get lost? How old were you? Did you get scared? What happened in the end?
4. A time you saw a celebrity. When and where was it? Who did you see? What was the celebrity doing? What was he or she wearing? Did you have a chance to speak to the celebrity?

SPORTS

DESCRIBE THE PICTURES AND ANSWER THE QUESTIONS

1. Which of these sports do you think is the most demanding physically?
2. Do you like any of these sports? What other sports do you like?
3. Why is sport important for our health?
4. Are there any sports more suitable for men and women in your opinion?

Work in pairs

ASK EACH OTHER THE FOLLOWING QUESTIONS.

1. Would you like to be a sports referee? Why? Why not?
2. Is cheating in sports considered a serious problem in your country?
3. Do you think sportsmen earn too much?
4. Do you consider sports a real job, vocation or just a hobby?

SPORTS

DESCRIBE THE PICTURES AND ANSWER THE QUESTIONS

1. How do you think sport makes these men feel?
2. Do you think disabled people in your country have enough support from the government?
3. What are the main causes of disability in your opinion?

Situational English

TALK TO YOUR COACH ABOUT AN UNPLEASANT SITUATION AND ASK HIM FOR HEP.

- Inform the coach you have been bullied by a member of the sports team.
- Tell him who the bully is, how long has it been going on and what exactly does the person do.
- Tell him you are scared of the repercussions.
- Ask him what he thinks you need to do.
- Thank him for the advice.

Situational English

YOU ARE CALLING A LOCAL GYM TO GET TO KNOW WHAT TRAINING PLANS THEY CAN OFFER.

- Introduce yourself.
- Say why you are calling and ask the gym worker to help you choose the best option for you.
- Say what your training goals are and how often you are planning to attend the gym.
- Ask for the price.
- Choose one option and enroll to the gym.

SPORTS
DESCRIBE THE PICTURE AND ANSWER THE QUESTIONS

1. Do you think the women are enjoying themselves? Why? Why not?
2. Would you like to try doing similar exercises in the open air? Why? Why not?
3. What do you think is the best physical activity that helps women to stay fit?

1. Why do people do extreme sports? Do you find extreme sports enjoyable to do or watch?
2. What other examples of extreme sports can you think of? Would you like to try any?
3. In case of an accident, who do you think should pay for the treatment if a person gets hurt while doing extreme sports?

SPORTS

DESCRIBE THE PICTURE AND ANSWER THE QUESTIONS

1. Do you think it is important to encourage children to do sports? Why?
2. Do you think children spend too much or too little time doing sports at school?
3. What are your earliest childhood memories connected with sport?
4. If you could be a champion at any sport which one would you choose and why?

Work in pairs

ASK EACH OTHER THE FOLLOWING QUESTIONS.

1. What was the first team sport you learnt to play when you were a child?
2. Do you like getting extremely tired while doing sports? Why? Why not?
3. When was the last time you enjoyed doing a sports activity?
4. Do you prefer exercising on your own or with other people? Why?
5. If you were to make a new year's resolution concerning your attitude towards sports, what would that be?
6. How do you think professional sports people start their day?
7. Do you know any famous sports people in person?

SPORTS

WORK IN PAIRS. LOOK AT THE PICTURES. NAME SPORTS AND THE ITEMS OF EQUIPMENT THAT ARE USED FOR A PARTICULAR DISCIPLINE.

Hurry up
WITHIN TWO MINUTES WRITE DOWN AS MANY NAMES OF SPORTSMEN AS YOU CAN REMEMBER. COMPARE THE LIST WITH A PARTNER AND EXPLAIN WHAT EACH PERSON IS FAMOUS FOR.

63

SPORTS TABOO

DESCRIBE THE WORD IN CAPITAL LETTERS WITHOUT USING THE WORDS IN LOWER CASE.

DANCE music move partner	**TENNIS** ball backhand forehand	**PLAYER** game men team
CYCLING bike wheels brake	**SWIMMING** pool water style	**FOOTBALL** men ball 11 players
FISHING fish water rod	**GOLF** club ball grass	**SKIING** skis snow winter
BOXING fight ropes belt	**HOCKEY** ice rink stick	**RUGBY** ball brutal team

SCIENCE AND TECHNOLOGY

DESCRIBE THE PICTURE AND ANSWER THE QUESTIONS

1. Have you ever tried the VR technology? What is your opinion about this type of entertainment?
2. Do you think children spend too much time playing games? What might be the consequences?

Work in pairs

DISCUSS AND DECIDE. ARE THESE SCIENTIFIC FACTS OR MYTHS? USE THE INTERNET TO SEARCH FOR ANSWERS.

1. Rubber tyres protect a car from lightning.
2. Antibiotics don't kill viruses.
3. Bats are blind.
4. Cracking your knuckles frequently increases your chance of developing arthritis.
5. Lightning never strikes the same place twice.
6. Bulls become angry when they see the color red.
7. The north star is the brightest star in the night sky.
8. The Great Wall of China is the only man-made thing visible from space.
9. Ostriches stick their heads into the ground when threatened.
10. Mice love cheese.
11. All dinosaurs went extinct by an asteroid hitting earth.
12. We only use ten per cent of our brains.
13. A full moon makes people and animals go mad.
14. There is no part of the moon which is permanently dark.
15. Albert Einstein was very bad at maths at school.

SCIENCE AND TECHNOLOGY

DESCRIBE THE PICTURE AND ANSWER THE QUESTIONS

1. Who do you think these people are to each other? What makes you think so?
2. Do you think technology facilitates or hinders communication? What has changed in interpersonal relations over the last few years?
3. How do you prefer to communicate with family and friends?

Work in pairs

ASK EACH OTHER THE FOLLOWING QUESTIONS.

1. Did you enjoy science lessons at school? What was your favourite subject and why? Was there any subject you hated?
2. Which scientific subject has taught you something useful? What was it?
3. What do you think is the most important scientific discovery of recent years? Why?
4. Are there any discoveries you wish hadn't been made? Why?
5. If you were ill, would you agree to try experimental treatment?
6. Are you happy to eat genetically modified food? Why? Why not?
7. Are you worried about any of the things scientists are currently experimenting with? Why? Why not?
8. What would you most like scientists to discover in the future?
9. Is it acceptable for animals to be used in experiments? Why? Why not?

SCIENCE AND TECHNOLOGY

DESCRIBE THE PICTURES AND ANSWER THE QUESTIONS

1. At what age do you think children should be introduced to technology?
2. What are some advantages and disadvantages of children using technology very early on? Does it influence their development in any way?
3. Should parents supervise how their kids use mobiles, computers, etc.?
4. Do you think children nowadays have different childhood than the previous generations had? What are the differences?

Work in pairs

DISCUSS AND DECIDE. ARE THE FOLLOWING SENTENCES TRUE OR FALSE? USE THE INTERNET TO SEARCH FOR ANSWERS.

1. When we breathe out, most of that is oxygen.
2. Pluto is no longer considered to be a planet in our solar system.
3. A diamond can be destroyed by intense heat.
4. Adult giraffes remain standing all day.
5. The human brain can continue to live without oxygen for nearly six minutes.
6. In direct current, the electrons move in only one direction.

SCIENCE AND TECHNOLOGY

DESCRIBE THE PICTURE AND ANSWER THE QUESTIONS

1. How do you think the woman would feel if she lost her phone?
2. Have you ever lost your phone? How did it happen?
3. What do you use your smartphone for? What other gadgets lost popularity with the development of a smartphone?
4. Can you imagine life without a smartphone? Why? Why not?
5. Do you think you suffer from information overload at times? If yes, what do you do then?

Work in pairs

DISCUSS THE QUESTIONS WITH A PARTNER.

1. How many devices do you have with screens? What do you use them for?
2. Do you prefer to use a keyboard with or without a mouse? Why?
3. Have you ever had to live without the internet for some time? Did you miss it?
4. What is the one device you could not live without? Why?
5. Would you like to live off the grid with no media, no electricity, etc.? Why? Why not?

SCIENCE AND TECHNOLOGY

DESCRIBE THE PICTURE AND ANSWER THE QUESTIONS

1. How much technology does the woman need in her everyday life? What for?
2. What are the pros and cons of working from home?
3. What, in your opinion, is the greatest technological invention ever, and why?
4. Is it possible to live without a smartphone nowadays? What would your life be like if you had no smartphone?

Situational English

A FRIEND OF YOURS NEEDS TO BUY SOME EQUIPMENT. THEY ASK YOU WHERE THE NEAREST SHOP IS.

- Ask what exactly they are looking for.
- Inform him or her where the nearest shop is and how to get there.
- Offer help with choosing the best equipment.

Situational English

YOU ARE BUYING A LAPTOP. TALK TO THE SHOP ASSISTANT.

- Tell the shop assistant what you are looking for.
- Ask what the shop has in stock and whether some products are reduced.
- Ask about the terms and conditions of a warranty.
- Buy the laptop that suits your needs.

SCIENCE AND TECHNOLOGY

DESCRIBE THE PICTURE AND ANSWER THE QUESTIONS

1. Do you think there is life on other planets?
2. What should governments do in case of a contact with aliens?
3. What do you think is the future of science? Will we be able to live on other planets?
4. Would you like to live in the space? Why? Why not?
5. What TV science programmes do you watch? Did you learn anything interesting?
6. Have you ever been to a science exhibition? What did it show? Did you enjoy it?

Situational English

YOU HAVE SEEN A VERY INTERESTING SCIENCE PROGRAMME ON TV. MENTION THE PROGRAMME WHILE TALKING TO A FRIEND.

- Say when was it on and why you decided to watch it.
- Describe what topics were presented.
- Give your opinion on the programme and the topics mentioned there.
- Encourage the friend to watch the programme too.

SCIENCE AND TECHNOLOGY

DESCRIBE THE PICTURES AND ANSWER THE QUESTIONS

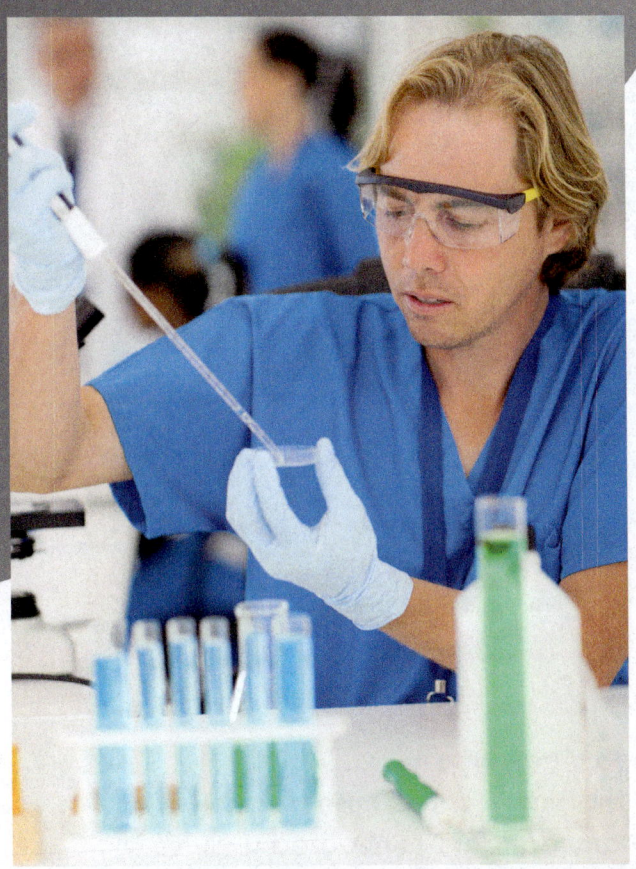

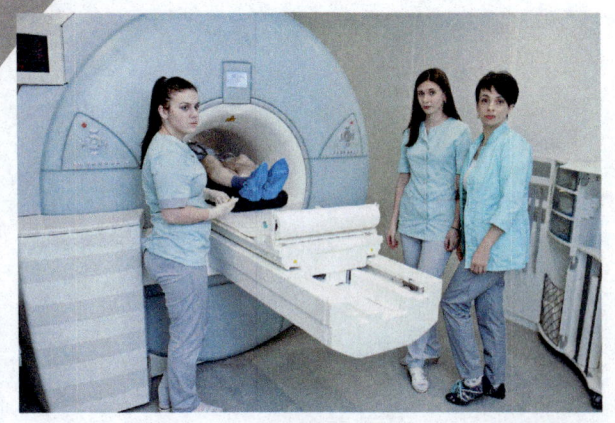

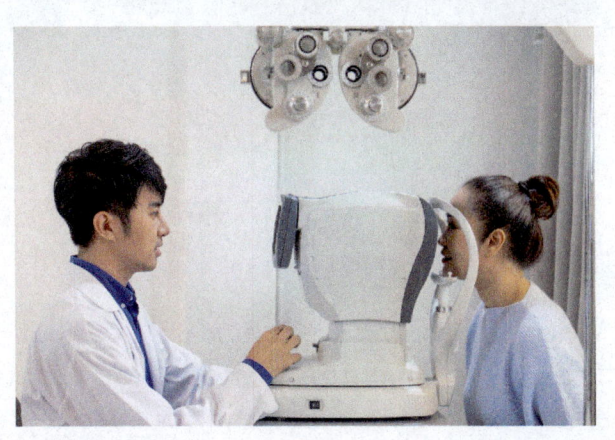

1. How does the technological development influence medicine?
2. What would medicine be like without technology?
3. What do you think is the most important technological invention that saves lives of many people?
4. Do you think we as people rely too much on technology? What makes you think so?
5. What do you think is the future of medicine? Are there any negative aspects of the changes?

---

1. What do you think is the future of AI?
2. Can AI be dangerous to people in any way?
3. Would you like technology to keep developing or stop developing? Why?
4. Why are some people afraid of technological progress?

SCIENCE AND TECHNOLOGY

DESCRIBE THE PICTURES AND ANSWER THE QUESTIONS

1. What can robots do that people cannot and vice versa?
2. Do you think is it possible to design robots that have consciousness and emotions? Do you find it ethical? Are there any dangers connected with it?
3. What will be the biggest human achievement in 2050?
4. Are you a fan of science fiction books or films? Why? Why not?
5. Describe the best science fiction film you have ever seen.

Work in pairs

DECIDE WHICH OF THE FOLLOWING INVENTIONS HAVE REVOLUTIONISED THE WORLD THE MOST.

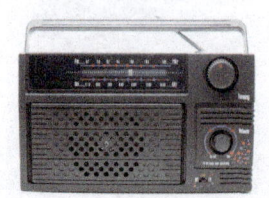

1. Which of the three inventions is the most important for you?
2. If you could choose only one object out of the three to keep, which one would you choose and why?
3. What piece of technology is completely useless for you? Why?
4. Would you like work as a scientist? Why? Why not?

SCIENCE AND TECHNOLOGY TABOO

DESCRIBE THE WORDS IN CAPITAL LETTERS. DO NOT USE THE WORDS IN LOWER CASE.

ROBOT metal not human alive	**AERIAL** TV radio wire	**SATNAV** drive way road
BULB light night Edison	**MOBILE** phone call text	**INTERNET** connection communication data
LAPTOP screen computer work	**ENGINE** fuel car water	**LASER** beam cut glow
PRINTER ink paper writing	**ASTRONOMY** study space universe	**MEDICINE** treat cure doctor

ENVIRONMENT AND NATURE

DESCRIBE THE PICTURE AND ANSWER THE QUESTIONS

1. What do you think about the conditions the animals are kept in?
2. Are you a fan of animals? What is your favourite animal?
3. Do you have any pets? What are the pros and cons of owning a pet?

Work in pairs

DISCUSS THE QUESTIONS WITH A PARTNER. WHAT WOULD YOU DO IF…?

1. you/ see/a mouse in the bedroom?
2. you/see/ someone being attacked by a stray dog?
3. you/see/ a huge spider in the bathroom?
4. someone/offer/you to buy a fur coat?
5. your neighbour's dog/bark/all night?
6. a wasp/fly/into your car while you are driving?
7. you/see/a shark very near you in the sea?
8. a poisonous snake/bite/you on the leg?
9. your friend/ask/you to look after his snake for the weekend?
10. you/are/serve/a kangaroo meat? Would you try it?

74

ENVIRONMENT AND NATURE
DESCRIBE THE PICTURE AND ANSWER THE QUESTIONS

1. Do you think the bear is happy being in captivity?
2. Is it fair to keep wild animals in cages? What are some justifiable reasons behind it?
3. Do you like visiting zoos? Describe the last time you were to a zoo?

Work in pairs

DISCUSS THE SENTENCES WITH A PARTNER. HOW PROBABLE IS IT THAT IN TWENTY YEARS' TIME...

1. Most people in the white collar sector will be working from home.
2. Most people will be using bikes to get to work.
3. People will live in energetically self-sufficient houses.
4. Fewer people will travel abroad.
5. The retirement age will be 70 or more.
6. People will have less face to face contact with each other.
7. Handwriting will be long forgotten.
8. People will live under constant surveillance.
9. Certain professions will not exist anymore.

ENVIRONMENT AND NATURE

DESCRIBE THE PICTURES AND ANSWER THE QUESTIONS

1. Name some renewable and non-renewable sources of energy. What are the pros and cons of using any of them?
2. What sources of energy are the safest for people and for the planet? What sources of energy are the most efficient?
3. What is your opinion about nuclear power plants? Can using nuclear energy be dangerous in any way?
4. Do you think climate changes can be stopped? If yes, how?

Work in pairs

DISCUSS THE HINTS WITH A PARTNER. DECIDE HOW ECO-GUILTY YOU ARE AND WHAT CAN YOU DO TO CHAGE IT.

1. I go by car everywhere. It is much more convenient than public transport.
2. I take a bath every day and leave the water running when I brush my teeth.
3. I shop at supermarkets. Local farmer's markets are too expensive.
4. I wash my clothes immediately after I use them even when they are not dirty.
5. I buy a new plastic bag every time I do shopping.

ENVIRONMENT AND NATURE

DESCRIBE THE PICTURES AND ANSWER THE QUESTIONS

1. What other natural disasters can you think of?
2. What are natural disasters caused by? Can anything be done to prevent them from happening?
3. Do natural disasters happen in your country? Describe the most recent one.
4. What do you think people who lose their homes due to a floor or a fire need the most?

Work in pairs

ASK EACH OTHER THE QUESTIONS.

1. What do you do to help protect the environment?
2. Why do you think so many people do not care about the environment?
3. What are the main difficulties when it comes to recycling materials?
4. What do you think about wearing clothes made from animals?
5. Do you believe our climate is changing? Why? Why not?

ENVIRONMENT AND NATURE

DESCRIBE THE PICTURES AND ANSWER THE QUESTIONS

1. What are the main causes of pollution?
2. Which industries are the biggest polluters?
3. What can be done to reduce pollution?
4. Is pollution a big problem in your area?

Work in pairs

ASK EACH OTHER THE QUESTIONS.

1. What is the best region in the world to live in?
2. What is the influence of deforestation on the environment?
3. How would you describe the weather in your country throughout the year?
4. What do you like and dislike about each season of the year?
5. If you could change weather conditions at will what changes would you make all over the world?
6. Describe the last time bad weather spoilt your plans.
7. How does the weather affect people's mood?

ENVIRONMENT AND NATURE

DESCRIBE THE PICTURE AND ANSWER THE QUESTIONS

1. What are the advantages and disadvantages of living in such a place?
2. Would you like to live in a small community?
3. Do you think such places will eventually disappear from the map? Why? Why not?

Work in pairs

DISCUSS THE SENTENCES WITH A PARTNER. HOW PROBABLE IS IT THAT IN FIFTY YEARS' TIME...

1. Most people will have solar panels and wind turbines installed on their houses to generate energy.
2. 100% of waste will be recycled.
3. Only electric cars will be allowed.
4. Robots will be used in majority of work places.
5. Paper books will no longer be produced to save trees.
6. Drinking water will be obtained from salt water.
7. Most glaciers will have melted due to tremendous rise in temperature worldwide.
8. Weather will be more extreme. Natural disasters will happen more frequently.

SCHOOL

DESCRIBE THE PICTURE AND ANSWER THE QUESTIONS

1. Do you think the students are enjoying the lesson? Why?
2. Did you like school? What are your best and worst memories?
3. What was your favourite subject and why? What subject did you struggle with?

Work in pairs

ASK AND ANSWER THE QUESTIONS.

1. Do you think being a teacher is a difficult job?
2. What are the main problems of teachers nowadays?
3. What are the main reasons for students to misbehave?
4. Do same-sex schools help to build a healthy society?
5. Did you study a lot as a student?
6. What was your favourite teacher like?
7. Do you think students should be given any homework at all?
8. What are the qualities of a good teacher?
9. What is your opinion about boarding schools?
10. Should pupils be punished for having bad marks?

SCHOOL

DESCRIBE THE PICTURE AND ANSWER THE QUESTIONS

1. Why do you think the students are studying together?
2. Do you prefer to study on your own or in company?
3. Describe educational system in your country. Do you think the system is effective?
4. What would you change in education if you could, and why?
5. Is learning by heart ever useful? How else can you remember what you learn?

Situational English

YOU ARE ORGANISING A SCHOOL REUNION TWENTY YEARS AFTER THE GRADUATION. YOU ARE CALLING A FORMER CLASSMATE TO INVITE HIM OR HER TO THE PARTY.

- Introduce yourself and remind the classmate where you know each other from.
- Inform him or her you are organising the special reunion party.
- Invite the classmate politely.
- Give exact details of where and when the event is going to take place.
- Give details concerning a dress code and the list of guests.
- Inform the classmate what food is going to be served. Ask about any food allergies.

SCHOOL

DESCRIBE THE PICTURES AND ANSWER THE QUESTIONS

IMAGINE YOU NEED TO PREPARE FOR A VERY IMPORTANT EXAM. WHICH WAY OF STUDYING, DO YOU THINK, WOULD BE THE MOST SUITABLE FOR YOU? WHY WOULD YOU REJECT THE OTHER TWO?

IMAGINE YOU WANT TO JOIN A SCHOOL CLUB. WHICH OF THE THREE WOULD YOU LIKE TO JOIN AND WHY? WHY WOULD YOU REJECT THE OTHER TWO OPTIONS?

SCHOOL

DESCRIBE THE PICTURE AND ANSWER THE QUESTIONS

1. What class do you think the students are taking? What makes you think so?
2. Describe the level of higher education in your country.
3. Is a degree necessary to get a well paid job in your country?
4. Are there any fields of study that give students satisfaction but do not give them job security?

Work in pairs

ASK AND ANSWER THE QUESTIONS

1. What do you think about learning online only? Would it be beneficial for the society? What advantages and disadvantages of online classes can you think of?
2. Is it possible to learn a language, a subject or a skill through playing games?
3. Do you think students work better in small classes? Why is that?
4. What are the tendencies in terms of education in your country? Do more or less people pursue higher education compared with the previous generation?
5. Do you think regular tests motivate students to study harder? Why? Why not?
6. Do you prefer written or spoken exams?

SCHOOL

DESCRIBE THE PICTURES AND ANSWER THE QUESTIONS

1. Why do you think the child looks discouraged?
2. Should parents be helping their children with doing homework? How did the trend change over the years?

1. Do you think the children are having a good day? Why Why not?
2. What are the advantages and disadvantages of compulsory uniforms at school? Do you think children should be allowed to wear what they want to school? What about jewellery, colourful hair, etc.?

SCHOOL

DESCRIBE THE PICTURES AND ANSWER THE QUESTIONS

1. What kind of book do you think the man is looking for?
2. Do you think that bookshops and libraries will disappear soon?
3. Do you like reading books? What is your favourite genre?

1. Do you think the children are enjoying the lesson?
2. At what age do you think children should start education?
3. What are the pros and cons of homeschooling? Is it better than conventional schooling in any way?

SCHOOL

DESCRIBE THE PICTURES AND ANSWER THE QUESTIONS

1. What do you think they are feeling right now?
2. Describe your graduation. Was it an important day for you?

1. What is your earliest memory connected with school?
2. Do you think you could be a nursery teacher? Why? Why not?

POLITICS AND SOCIETY

DESCRIBE THE PICTURES AND ANSWER THE QUESTIONS

1. Is patriotism popular and valued in your country?
2. Do you consider yourself a patriot? What do you love your country for?

1. Are female politicians popular in your country? Why? Why not?
2. Have you ever considered taking up politics? Why? Why not?

POLITICS AND SOCIETY

DESCRIBE THE PICTURES AND ANSWER THE QUESTIONS

1. Is homelessness a problem in your country?
2. What are the main causes of homelessness?
3. In what ways can the government and the ordinary people help the homeless?

1. Do you think war is ever justifiable? Why? Why not?
2. Is there anything THE ordinary people can do to stop wars? Why? Why not?

POLITICS AND SOCIETY

DESCRIBE THE PICTURE AND ANSWER THE QUESTIONS

1. What do you think is the relation between the people in the picture?
2. Is harassment a big issue in your country? Do victims get enough support?
3. What would you do if you were a witness of a crime?

Work in pairs

DISCUSS THE TOPICS WITH A PARTNER.

1. Every government should put a limit on immigration.
2. Benefits for the disabled should be higher.
3. The problem of homelessness should be dealt with more effectively.
4. Rasism should be defined worldwide and severely punished.
5. The government should take measures to combat unemployment.
6. Discrimination against women is still an issue in many places in the world.
7. Lack of basic education is the main cause of extreme poverty.
8. Death penalty should be abolished.
9. Resocialisation very rarely works properly.
10. Countries that break human rights should be sanctioned.

POLITICS AND SOCIETY

DESCRIBE THE PICTURE AND ANSWER THE QUESTIONS

1. What do you think had happened before the picture was taken?
2. Is being a fire fighter a difficult job? Why? Why not?
3. Have you ever considered becoming a fire fighter? Why? Why not?

Work in pairs

ASK AND ANSWER THE QUESTIONS WITH A PARTNER.

1. Do you follow politics? Why? Why not?
2. Is politics a taboo topic in your country?
3. In what ways do the politicians in your country do a good job? In what ways are they disappointing?
4. What things do people usually say about politicians? Do you agree or disagree with those ideas?
5. Has your country ever had a female leader? Why do men dominate politics in most nations?
6. What social and economic issues divide the people in your country?
7. Is ethnicity or race a factor in the politics in your country? How so?
8. Is environmentalism an important factor in politics in your country? Is there a political party that is focused on green issues?

POLITICS AND SOCIETY

DESCRIBE THE PICTURES AND ANSWER THE QUESTIONS

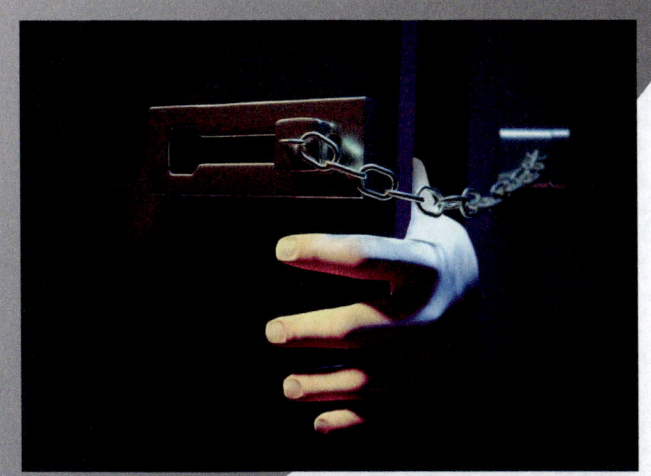

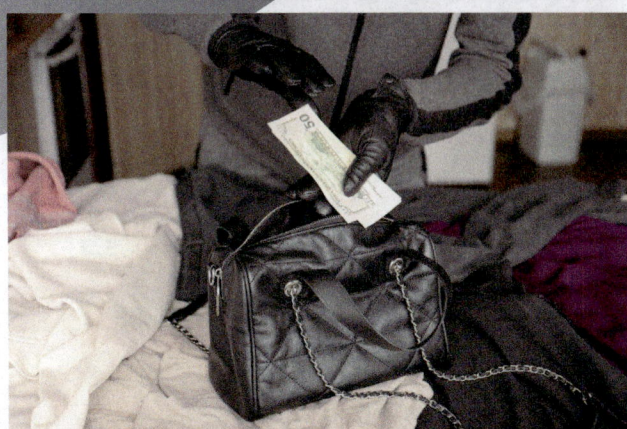

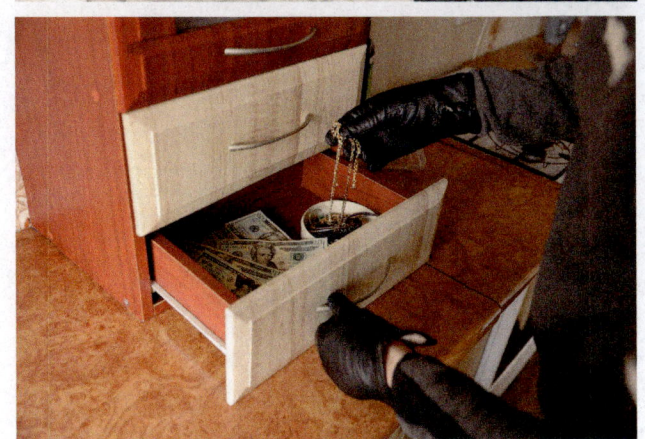

1. How do you think the burglar opened the door?
2. How long do you think an averge burglar takes to search someone's house?
3. Which are the most common things that burglars steal?
4. How are burglars most likely to get into a house?
5. What can be done to deter burglars from targeting your home?
6. How do you think burglars pick up targets?
7. Why do you think some burglars prefer it if the owner is at home?
8. When are you most likely to get burgled?
9. Have you or anyone you know ever been robbed in the street?
10. What rules do people need to stick to in order to avoid being robbed?
11. Do rich people get away with crimes? Is the system unfair?
12. Do you enjoy television shows about crime and the police? Which ones are good?
13. Is there legal behavior in your country that you think should be made illegal?
14. Is the overall crime rate increasing or decreasing where you live? Do you think the world will be safer or more dangerous in the future?
15. How can we reduce crime? With harsher punishments or better education?
16. If a person acts in self-defense and accidentally hurts someone, should they be punished?
17. At what age are we fully responsible for our actions? What is the youngest age that a criminal should be punished as an adult?
19. How do you feel about drunk driving? What is the proper punishment for someone who drinks alcohol and drives?

POLITICS AND SOCIETY

DESCRIBE THE PICTURE AND ANSWER THE QUESTIONS

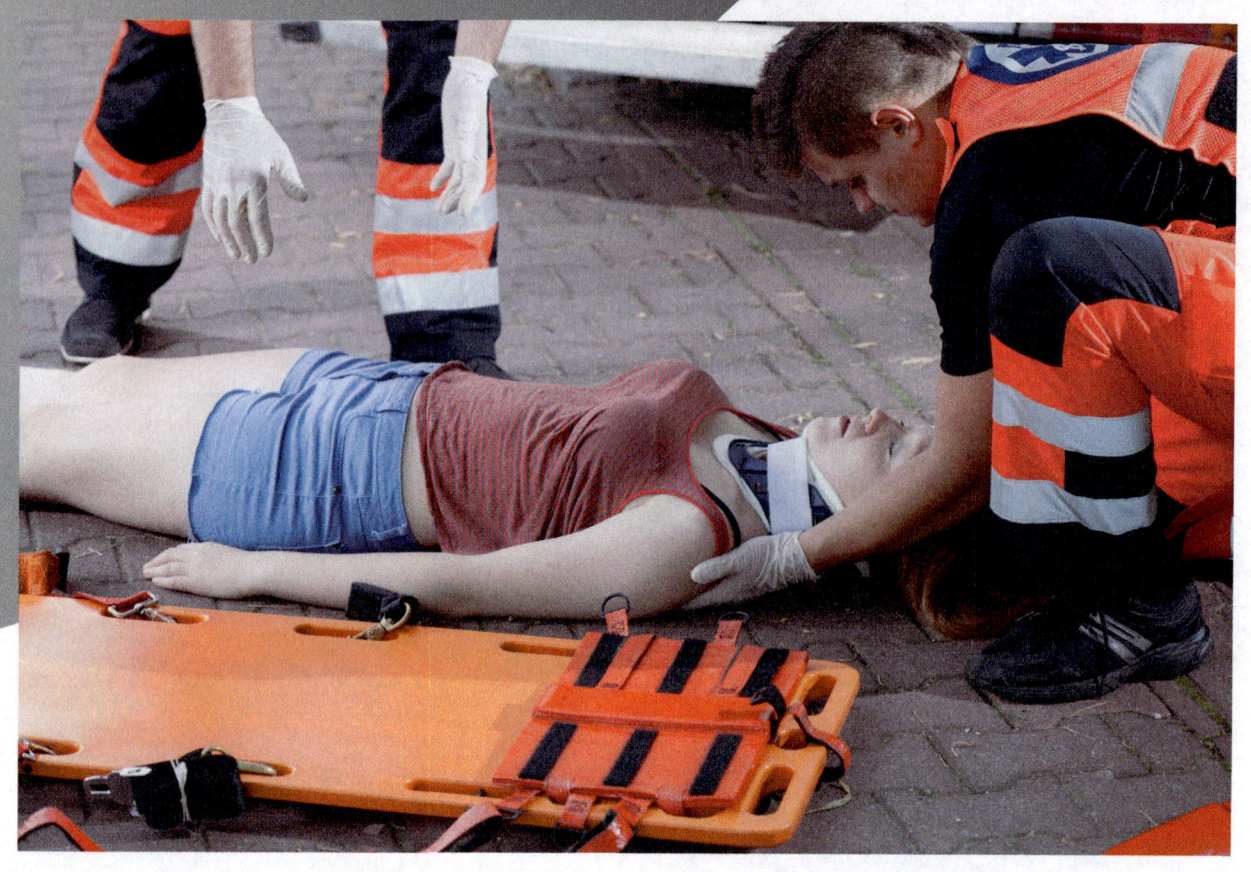

1. What do you think had happened before the picture was taken?
2. Do you know how to give first aid? Describe a situation when you or someone you know had to give first aid.
3. What are the main causes of injuries people suffer from?

Work in pairs

ASK AND ANSWER THE QUESTIONS WITH A PARTNER.

1. What role does religion play in the politics of your country?
2. In your opinion, what is the most important issue your country is facing? What could be done to improve the situation?
3. Do the politics of another country affect your life in any way? Are your politicians doing a good job dealing with it?
4. Is war a form a politics? Or is politics a form of war?
5. Do politics influence interpersonal relations? Can you be friends with someone if they have very different political views from you?
6. Do you have a favorite political leader? What did they do?

POLITICS AND SOCIETY

DESCRIBE THE PICTURE AND ANSWER THE QUESTIONS

1. Why do you think the man is getting arrested?
2. Do you feel safe where you live? What could be done to improve safety in your country?
3. What are the most infamous crimes people commit in your country? Why do you think they do it?

Work in pairs

DISCUSS HOW YOU UNDERSTAND THE FOLLOWING AFRICAN PROVERS.

1. Knowledge without wisdom is like water in the sand. Guinean Proverb
2. Examine what is said, not him who speaks. Egyptian Proverb
3. A canoe does not know who the leader is, when it turns over, everyone gets wet. Madagascar Proverb
4. An empty pot makes the loudest noise. Kenyan Proverb
5. We should put out fire while it is still small. Kenyan Proverb
6. If you damage the character of someone else, you damage your own. Yoruba Proverb
7. A snake that you see does not bite. Mozambican Proverb
8. One who relates with a corrupt person likewise gets corrupted. Kenyan Proverb

POLITICS AND SOCIETY

DESCRIBE THE PICTURES AND ANSWER THE QUESTIONS

1. Why do you think people become criminals?
2. Have you or anyone you know had anything stolen? What was it?
3. Why do you think so many people are violent these days?

1. What would you do if witnessed an act of vandalism? Would you react? Why? Why not?
2. Is vandalism as issue in your country?
3. Describe a crime that has been in the news recently.

POLITICS AND SOCIETY

DESCRIBE THE PICTURE AND ANSWER THE QUESTIONS

1. Why do you think the child is in a basement?
2. If someone's home gets burned or flooded, what help can they expect from the government in your country? Is the support sufficient?
3. What could be done all over the world to prevent war?
4. What is your opinion concerning humanitarian aid to refugees? What is the best way to help?

Work in pairs

DISCUSS HOW YOU UNDERSTAND THE FOLLOWING AFRICAN PROVERS.

1. Numbers can achieve anything.
2. What is bad luck for one man is good luck for another.
3. Tomorrow belongs to people who prepare for it today.
4. If you think you're too small to make a difference, try spending the night with a mosquito.
5. A fool has to say something. A wise person has something to say.
6. To get lost is to learn the way.
7. If you want to go quickly, go alone. If you want to go far, go together.

POLITICS AND SOCIETY

DESCRIBE THE PICTURES AND ANSWER THE QUESTIONS

1. What do you think the press conference is about?
2. Are politicians in your country respected and trusted? Why? Why not?
3. Do you think politics is easy? Is it for everyone?

1. What do you think is the man's role in the country? What makes you think so?
2. Were you to be the president of your country, what changes would you introduce?

POLITICS AND SOCIETY

DESCRIBE THE PICTURES AND ANSWER THE QUESTIONS

1. What do you think the protesters are protesting against?
2. Do you think protesting is the correct way to induce changes?
3. What would need to happen to make you join a protest?

1. Is bribery an issue in your country?
2. What are some reasons why people may consider trying to bribe a politician, a police officer, a doctor, etc.?

SHOPPING AND FASHION

DESCRIBE THE PICTURE AND ANSWER THE QUESTIONS

1. Why do you think the woman decided to do her shopping there?
2. Do you prefer shopping in large supermarkets or small local shops?
3. What are your favourite grocery stores? Why do you do shopping there?

Work in pairs

DISCUSS WITH A PARTNER IF YOU AGREE WITH THE FOLLOWING STATEMENTS.

1. What people wear says a lot about their lifestyle and personality.
2. We should not judge people by the way they look.
3. Expensive clothes last longer.
4. People who follow fashion are usually vain.
5. Buying clothes online can go wrong.
6. Fashion industry promotes wrong image of health and moral code.
7. Women tend to focus more on fashion than men.
8. Sales are often scams.
9. People tend to buy too much food nowadays.
10. Most men do not like shopping for clothes.

SHOPPING AND FASHION

DESCRIBE THE PICTURE AND ANSWER THE QUESTIONS

1. Do you think the women are enjoying shopping together? What makes you say so?
2. Do you prefer shopping for clothes alone or accompanied by friends?
3. What is the best way to save money while doing shopping?

Work in pairs

ASK AND ANSWER THE FOLLOWING QUESTIONS WITH A PARTNER.

1. What is the role of jewellery in our society?
2. How is bargaining perceived in your culture? Can you bargain?
3. What is your favourite shop to buy clothes and why?
4. What do you enjoy and hate buying?
5. Have you ever spent too much money while doing shopping? What did you buy? How did you feel afterwards?
6. How long do you usually shop for? Do you try to get your shopping done as fast as possible?
7. Do you shop online? What kind of things do you buy online? What would you rather buy in person?
8. Think about the most expensive thing you have ever bought. Was it worth what you paid for it?
9. Who does the grocery shopping in your household? How often do they do it?
10. Which do you prefer? Buying things for yourself or for other people?

SHOPPING AND FASHION

DESCRIBE THE PICTURE AND ANSWER THE QUESTIONS

1. What are the qualities of a good sales person?
2. Have you ever considered working in a shop? Do you think you would make an efficient sales person?

Work in pairs

ASK AND ANSWER THE FOLLOWING QUESTIONS WITH A PARTNER.

1. Are you a bargain hunter? Do you get excited about sales and discounts? When are the best sales in your country?
2. Do you collect points or stamps at any stores?
3. Is shoplifting a big issue in your country? What can shops do to prevent it?
4. Have you or anyone you know had anything stolen while you were doing shopping?
5. What can you do to deter pickpokets?
6. Have you ever worked in a shop? What was the store selling? Does that kind of job suit you?
7. If you were to open your own shop, what kind of things would you like to sell?

SHOPPING AND FASHION

DESCRIBE THE PICTURES AND ANSWER THE QUESTIONS

1. What is the legal age for consumption of alcohol in your country? Do you think the age limit is set properly?
2. Does your country struggle with alcoholism? What can be done to prevent it?

1. Do you think local food markets offer better quality products than supermarkets?
2. Where do you like to do your grocery shopping and why?

SHOPPING AND FASHION

WORK IN PAIRS. EACH PERSON GETS THEIR OWN PICTURE. PERSON "A" DESCRIBES THEIR PICTURE. PERSON "B" CIRCLES THE DIFFERENCES AND COMPARES THE PICTURES.

SHOPPING AND FASHION

WORK IN PAIRS. EACH PERSON GETS THEIR OWN PICTURE. PERSON "B" DESCRIBES THEIR PICTURE. PERSON "A" CIRCLES THE DIFFERENCES AND COMPARES THE PICTURES.

1.

2.

SHOPPING AND FASHION

DESCRIBE THE PICTURES AND ANSWER THE QUESTIONS

1. Does your country struggle with unemployment? What can be done to improve the situation?
2. Describe a situation when you met a very helpful shopping assistant.

1. What are the advantages and disadvantages for paying by card and using cash for customers, shop owners and shop assistants?
2. Do you prefer to use cash or card and why?
3. Do you think cash will disappear soon? What makes you think so?
4. Why do teenagers like hanging out in shopping malls so much?
5. What attracts you to buying things most?
6. What facilities a make shopping centre popular?
7. Should shops be open on Sundays? Why? Why not?

SHOPPING AND FASHION

DESCRIBE THE PICTURE AND ANSWER THE QUESTIONS

1. Are comic book shops and music shops popular in your country? Do you like visiting such places? Why? Why not?
2. If you were to open a shop what you would be selling and why?
3. How did lockdowns influence local businesses in your area? What are some solutions people should implement to improve their financial situation?

Work in pairs

IMAGINE YOU CAN INVEST A SUBSTANTIAL SUM OF MONEY IN ONE OF THE FOLLOWING PRODUCTS. WHICH PRODUCT WOULD YOU CHOOSE TO INVEST IN AND WHY? WHAT ARGUMENTS WOULD YOU USE TO ADVERTISE IT?

1. Clothes that never need to be washed
2. Cars that run on water
3. Pills that can substitute food
4. Pills that help people fight with any addiction
5. A platform where people's avatars can travel in space and time
6. Special locks that make your door inpenetrable
7. Air purifier that allows you to breathe clean air even in the most polluted environment

THE MEDIA

DESCRIBE THE PICTURES AND ANSWER THE QUESTIONS

1. Why do you think the people are recording what they are doing?
2. What is the role of social media in today's world?
3. Would you agree that more and more people live by observing others rather than by experiencing life themselves? Why do you think it is?
4. Do you follow any celebrities on social media? Why? Why not?
5. What do you think about influencers? What is thier influence on youngsters? Should they be held accountable for the type of content they present?
6. How did people socialise before the outbreak of social media apps?
7. Is advertising a business on social media helpful? What do you think is the best way to gather followers?
8. Have you ever considered starting an online business? Were you to start one, what would it be and why?
9. Which parts of our lives will never be online?
10. Have you ever met anyone online and then met them in person? Was the person like you expected them to be?
11. Have you ever played online games? What did you play?
12. Have you tried online dating? What are some pros and cons of online dating?
13. What are some safety tips for online dating?
14. What is your favorite smartphone app? What does it allow you to do?
15. What social media do you use these days? Why do you prefer those over other social networks?

THE MEDIA

DESCRIBE THE PICTURE AND ANSWER THE QUESTIONS

1. Do you prefer reading newspapers online or in a paper version? Why?
2. How do you find out the latest news?
3. Which sections of a newspaper do you usually read and which do you usually skip? Relationships? Politics? Weather? Sports? Celebrity gossip? News?
4. What are the most popular papers and magazines in your country? Why are they so popular?
5. Are there any titles that used to be very popular but they disappeared from the market due to the Internet?

Situational English

YOUR INTERNET CONNECTION IS DOWN. YOU ARE CALLING THE PROVIDER'S HELP LINE.

- Introduce yourself and say why you are calling.
- Describe the problem and say how long it has been going on.
- Ask if there is anything that can be done on your end.
- Arrange a technician's appointment.
- Thank the customer service worker and end the call politely.

THE MEDIA

DESCRIBE THE PICTURE AND ANSWER THE QUESTIONS

1. Who do you think the woman is?
2. How do you think she is feeling at the moment?
3. What are the advantages and disadvantages of being famous?
4. Do you think it is easy for celebrities to avoid paparazzi?
5. Is there a need to have stricter laws to protect people from paparazzi?

Work in pairs
ASK AND ANSWER THE FOLLOWING QUESTIONS WITH A PARTNER.

1. Would you like to be famous? What would you like to be famous for?
2. Who are the most famous people around the world? What do they do that makes them famous?
3. Who is someone that is famous only in your region or country? What are they known for?
4. Are famous people usually good looking? Who does not fit this stereotype?
5. People are interested in the lives of famous people. Is this okay, or should people mind their own business?
6. It can seem like there is advertising everywhere. Does it bother you? Do you notice it?

THE MEDIA

DESCRIBE THE PICTURES AND ANSWER THE QUESTIONS

1. What are the desireable qualities of a news reporter?
2. Would you like to work for the media? Why? Why not? If yes, would it be a newspaper, TV, social media? Why?
3. Do you think media can be trusted these days? What makes you say so?
4. Is there censorship in your country? Should news be allowed to state what they want to state?
5. Imagine you are responsible for inventing a new journalism entical code. What 5 rules can you think of?

---

1. Who do you think the people are to each other? What makes you think so?
2. Do you like taking photos? Why? Why not?
3. Do you think it is possible to make money on photography?
4. Are photographers artists?
5. Is photography a popular hobby in your country?

CULTURE

DESCRIBE THE PICTURES AND ANSWER THE QUESTIONS

1. What film, do you think, the people are watching? What makes you think so?
2. Do you like going to the cinema or do you prefer watching films at home? What are the pros and cons of both?
3. Is going to the cinema a popular past time activity in your country?
4. Who are the most popular actors in your country? What are they famous for? Do you think they are good role models for the youngsters?

1. What kind of play do you think the actors are performing and why?
2. Is theatre popular in your country? Why? Why not?
3. How has the entertainment industry changed over the years?
4. What kind of people do you think enjoy the so called "high culture"?

CULTURE

DESCRIBE THE PICTURES AND ANSWER THE QUESTIONS

1. Which countries or cultures do you associate the pictures with?
2. What makes your culture distinguishable?
3. Do you think globalisation causes national traits to die out?
4. In your opinion which one is better- having multiple national countries or having one huge conglomerate association?

Work in pairs

DISCUSS HOW YOU UNDERSTAND THE FOLLOWING NATIVE AMERICAN PROVERS AND SAYINGS.

1. All flowers of all the tomorrows are in the seeds today.
2. Tell me and I will forget, show me and I may not remember. Involve me, and I will understand.
3. Certain things catch your eye, but pursue only the things that capture the heart.
4. Seek wisdom, not knowledge. Knowledge is of the past, wisdom is of the future.
5. The one who tells the stories rules the world.
6. When you were born you cried and the world rejoiced. Live your life so that when you die, the world cries and you rejoice.
7. Don't let yesterday use up too much of today.
8. A danger foreseen is half-avoided.

CULTURE

DESCRIBE THE PICTURES AND ANSWER THE QUESTIONS

1. Which countries or cultures do you associate the pictures with?
2. Do you think enough has been done to protect the heritage of the indigenous peoples?
3. Would you like to spend some time living the life of some indigenous people? Why? Why not? Which people? What do you think you could learn form this expercience?

Work in pairs

DISCUSS HOW YOU UNDERSTAND THE FOLLOWING NATIVE AMERICAN PROVERS AND SAYINGS.

1. Those who lie down with dogs, get up with fleas.
2. You cannot wake a person who is pretending to be asleep.
3. When a man moves away from nature his heart becomes hard.
4. You already possess everything necessary to become great.
5. It is easy to be brave from a distance.
6. Day and night cannot dwell together.
7. Everyone who is successful must have dreamt of something.
8. We will be known forever by the tracks we leave.
9. Listen, or your tongue will make you deaf.
10. Cherish youth, but trust old age.

CULTURE

CINEMA QUIZZ

Describe a film that was incredibly funny
Describe a film that had a very sad ending
Describe a film that sent you to sleep
Describe a film that you have seen several times
Describe a film that made you buy the soundtrack
Do you prefer seeing films at home, or in the cinema?
Do you prefer watching American films or films from your own country?
Who is your favourite director and why?
Are there any scenes in films you avoid watching?
Which film star would you like to meet and what questions would you ask?
Which film has been widely advertised recently? Are you going to see it?
Do you prefer to read the book or see the film first?
Is there anything that frustrates you while watching a film in the cinema?
Describe a film that has been a waste of money
If you were to be a producer, what film would you like to release and why?

CULTURE

DESCRIBE THE PICTURES AND ANSWER THE QUESTIONS

1. How important, do you think, is the role of the film crew in making a film? Is the crew more important than the actors?
2. What do you pay attention to while watching a film? The script? The soundtrack? The play?
3. Have you ever considered becoming an actor? What qualities does a good actor need to have?
4. How important is it for children to have good role models?
5. What does the word 'hero' mean to you?
6. Who are the heroes of your country or culture according to most people? Do you agree that those people are heroes?
7. Do you have any personal heroes? What makes them special to you?
8. If a person does something impressive in science, sport or culture, should we consider them a hero?
9. What's the difference between a hero and a superhero?
10. Do you watch superhero movies? Why or why not?
11. If you could have one superhero power, which one would you want to have?
12. Who is your favorite superhero from comics books or movies? Why do you like them?
13. Who is your favorite villain from any movie? What makes them a great villain?
14. Are there real people in the world that seem like villains? Who are they?
15. Do you enjoy live music? Have you been to any concerts? Talk about the most memorable concert that you have been to.
16. What makes you like a song? The melody, the lyrics, or something else?

CULTURE

DESCRIBE THE PICTURES AND ANSWER THE QUESTIONS

1. Have you ever been the victim of discrimination?
2. Is racism common in your community? What forms of racist behavior have you noticed?
3. What stereotypes about people from different countries are you aware of?
4. 'Black Lives Matter' is a slogan and movement that started in the United States. What is it about?
5. Do certain racial groups have particular strengths or abilities? Is it wrong to point out these differences if they are basically positive qualities?
6. What are traditional male and female social roles and responsibilities? Are you a traditional person?
7. Do you trust men or women more in any particular profession? How do you feel about male nurses? How about a female president?
8. Women are on average paid less than men for doing the same job. Why is this?
9. What kind of discrimination do homosexual people face?
10. What do you think about gay marriage?
11. Should gay couples be allowed to adopt children?
12. Who suffers more discrimination on the basis of age? Old people or young people?
13. Are you a member of a religion? How does your religion treat members of other religions?
14. Which types of people do you think suffer the least discrimination?
15. Is the level of discrimination in the world rising or falling? What makes you think so?

MY NOTES

POWERPRINT PUBLISHERS

Printed in Great Britain
by Amazon